STEPHEN COLBERT

Beyond Truthiness

Bruce Watson

CHAPTER 1
STEPSON OF THE SOUTH

"I love the truth. It's the facts I'm not a fan of."

The president looked bewildered. The guests looked confused. The tuxedo-and-corsage crowd at the White House Correspondents' Association Dinner in 2006 expected the president to take a little ribbing, but no one expected *this*. The comedian at the podium looked harmless enough - clean-cut, bespectacled, much like a television anchorman - but had anyone watched his show? Did anyone know what a crazed character he pretended to be? Had *anyone* warned George W. Bush? The president leaned back in his chair, a look of disgust on his face, and let Stephen Colbert continue.

"Wow, what an honor! The White House Correspondents' dinner! To sit here at the same table with my hero, George W. Bush! To be this close to the man! I feel like I'm dreaming. Somebody pinch me! You know, I'm a pretty sound sleeper - that may not be enough. Somebody shoot me in the face." The vice president, who had recently shot a hunting partner by accident, was absent, but the president was not amused. Colbert, standing just ten feet from the most powerful man in the world, adjusted his glasses and pressed on.

"My name is Stephen Colbert, and tonight it is my privilege to celebrate this president because we're not so different, he and I. We both get it. Guys like us, we're not some brainiacs on the Nerd Patrol. We're not members of the Fact-inista." Bush's head bobbed as he chuckled, and Colbert turned to him. "We go straight from the gut, right, sir? That's where the truth lies - right down here in the gut. Ladies and gentlemen, do you know you have more nerve endings in your gut than you have in your head? You can look it up. Now I know some of you are going to tell me, 'I looked it up, and that's not true.' That's 'cause you looked it up in a book. Next time, look it up in your gut."

After a few jokes about believing in America – "I believe it exists; my gut tells me I live there" – Colbert turned to politics. "I believe the government that governs best is the government that governs least.

And by these standards, we have set up a fabulous government in Iraq." Getting his first big laugh, Colbert then aimed for the president's gut. Bush squirmed.

"Most of all, I believe in this president. Now I know there's some polls out there saying that this man has a 32 percent approval rating. But guys like us, we don't pay attention to the polls. We know that polls are just a collection of statistics that reflect what people are thinking in reality. And reality has a well-known liberal bias."

Laying on the sarcasm, spreading it with vainglorious gestures and pontifical patriotism, Colbert continued for another fifteen minutes. Laughter was sporadic. White House reporters were accustomed to sarcasm, but Colbert took aim at them, too, praising them for soft-peddling issues: tax cuts, weapons of mass destruction, global warming? "We Americans didn't want to know, and you had the courtesy not to try to find out," Colbert proclaimed.

Many reporters sat with grim faces or downcast looks, their bewilderment suggesting they were witnessing the crash landing of a career, not its takeoff. But within days, people in Washington and all of America were talking about the comedian who had the guts – or gut – to speak truth to oblivious power. Some of the comments included: "A battle cry from a court jester" (*Seattle Post Intelligencer*);

"The man is a genius" (*Philadelphia Inquirer*); and "One of the great satirical wits of our time" (*San Antonio Express News*).

Colbert's "Mocking of the President 2006" aired live only on C-SPAN and MSNBC. Deep in the cable wilderness, it may have attracted a sliver of the prime-time audience, but within days, the twenty-two-minute video became an Internet sensation. More than 2.7 million YouTube hits led C-SPAN to demand that the footage be removed. When the clip was shifted to Google Videos and a new Web site, thankyoustephencolbert.org, the hits kept coming. Released as an audio selection on iTunes, Colbert's attack instantly topped the download charts. "Stephen Colbert" became the Web's top search term. Gawker.com asked readers to vote whether the comedian had pulled off "one of the most patriotic acts I've witnessed" or was "not really that funny." Colbert was featured on *60 Minutes*, profiled in magazines and newspapers, and lauded as the man who finally made the truth "painful for President Bush, his cronies, and the media."

When he stepped before the president, Stephen Colbert was known mostly to cynics and skeptics - a man who would have been unwelcome at the White House. Today, he is the leader of an entire nation. Colbert Nation includes not just the 2 million Comedy Central viewers who watch *The Colbert Report* every night. This singular society, part fan club and part cult, has spread the pompous ego of Colbert's character around the world and into outer space.

Colbert has testified before Congress and twice run for president. He has sung with Paul McCartney, hung his portrait in the National Portrait Gallery, and inspired a "Google bombing" campaign that made colbertnation.com the first hit for those searching the terms "greatest living American" and "giant brass balls."

Making fun of celebrity culture, Colbert has encouraged his fans to lobby for the placement of his name on just about everything, resulting in "Stephen Colbert" appearing on an airliner, a spider, a Ben & Jerry's Ice Cream flavor, a nesting peregrine falcon, and a piece of the International Space Station.

But what's most interesting about Stephen Colbert is not who he is but who he isn't. To begin with, Stephen Colbert is not STEPHEN COLBERT! Off camera, the loudmouthed self-promoter turns into a gentle, polite father of three; a staunch Catholic and Sunday-school teacher; a lover of fantasy; a serious student of the works of J.R.R. Tolkien; and a major comedic artist whose career has been as finely tuned as his jokes.

So who is this faux-conservative comedian? This man who came from South Carolina but has no trace of an accent? Who gave up his dream of being a dramatic actor to struggle through the ranks of sketch comedy? Who, as a correspondent for Comedy Central's *The Daily Show,* deftly parodied the maudlin sincerity of news correspondents? Who, on the first episode of his own show, coined the word truthiness, the zeitgeist term of our times? Who simultaneously embodies and satirizes America's pompous celebrity culture? Who IS THIS COMEDIAN WHO takes nothing, not even the awesomeness of presidential power, seriously? And why doesn't he pronounce the "t" in his last name?

The family pronounces the name Colbert with a hard "t." Even before its youngest member became a celebrity, the name was said with pride. Colbert's father James climbed his way out of an Irish-Catholic boyhood in the Bronx to attend Columbia University Medical School. An army captain during World War II, he eventually became a leading specialist in epidemiology and the youngest medical school dean in the United States.

James Colbert was a model father, deeply involved with his children and his church, and devoted to his wife, Lorna. Stephen's mother grew up in New York's Westchester County in a well-to-do family. She spent summers in the Adirondacks and the rest of the year in a convent school in Rhode Island. During the Depression, Lorna Tuck met James Colbert at a cotillion.

Just twelve, but immediately smitten, she kept her crush to herself and waited. James began to notice the young woman with wavy brown hair and a Hollywood smile when she turned fifteen, and they began to date. Lorna dreamed of an acting career but gave it up when, after acting in college, she took sick and was bedridden for a year. Married in 1942, she became a professional mom. The couple had children, and children, and more children - James, Edward, Mary, Billy, Margo, Thomas, Jay, Elizabeth, Paul, Peter . . . and, finally, Stephen.

Stephen Colbert is the youngest of eleven children. All were fast-talking, funny, and fun. They made a party out of just being in the same room at the same time. "My brother Billy was the joke teller," Colbert recalled. "My brother Jim had a really sharp, cutting wit. And the teller of long stories, that was my brother Ed. As a child, I just absorbed everything they said, and I was always in competition for the laughs."

Colbert has often called his family a "humorocracy where the funniest person in the room is king." Yet the Colberts were also a highly-motivated, intellectual family. Dr. Colbert, Stephen once said, was "a big thinker, a true intellectual. His idea of a good time was to read French philosophy, often French-Christian philosophy."[1] Few dinners with the Colberts ended without quizzes from their father and theatrics from their mother.

Lorna Colbert, perhaps hoping to pass down her love of theater, encouraged her children to sing and act. "We were the light of her life," Colbert said. Lorna even taught each child to swoon on command, rolling to the floor. "We all learned how to do the falls," Colbert said. "And we'd fall all over the house, all the time, and my mom was fine with it." Stephen never forgot and was eternally grateful to Lorna for teaching him, despite the family's tragedies, to "love life without bitterness." When she was dying in June 2013, he took a week off from his show to be at her bedside in South Carolina. Finally, bidding her goodbye, he leaned over and said, "Mom, I'm going back to New York to do the show." And she said, "I can't wait to see it. I wouldn't miss it for the world."

Weeping, Colbert returned to tell all of Colbert Nation about his remarkable mother. "If you watch this show and you like this show, that's because of the wonderful people who work here," he began. "But when you watch the show and you also like me, that's because of my mom."

Reviewing her life, he choked up several times but paid her the ultimate tribute. "She was fun," he said. Pausing for a few seconds, he added, "It may sound greedy to want more days with a person who lived so long, but the fact that my mother was ninety-two does not diminish - it only magnifies - the enormity of the room whose door has now quietly shut."

Like the stage family Lorna longed to have, the Colberts took to the road regularly. In the years before Stephen was born, the family was uprooted several times following Dr. Colbert as he rose through the medical ranks. From New Haven, Connecticut, where he did his residency at Yale, the family moved to Germany where the Army stationed him, then back to New Haven where he advanced to assistant dean of the Yale Medical School.

Moving on to St. Louis, a few more Colberts were born while Dr. Colbert chaired the medical school at Washington University. Then, in the early 1960s, with ten children in tow, the family relocated to Bethesda, Maryland, where Dr. Colbert worked for the National Institutes of Health (NIH). While there, the lifelong Republican fell under the sway of a fellow Irishman, John F. Kennedy, for whom he and Lorna voted. A photo of Dr. Colbert shaking hands with President Kennedy soon became an icon in the Colbert house. And on May 13, 1964, while Dr. Colbert was working for the NIH, Stephen was born.

Five years later, the family made one more move to the charming old city of Charleston, South Carolina, where Dr. Colbert became the vice president for academic affairs at the Medical University of South Carolina.

By 1969, the civil rights movement was roiling the South, yet Charleston clung to its past.

De facto segregation and a deep economic divide prevailed throughout the city. Confederate flags flew. Elegant antebellum homes were tended by African-American servants. And two Charleston establishments, the military school known as The Citadel and Fort Sumter where the Civil War began, were constant reminders of the city's conservative, Confederate roots.

When the Colbert family arrived, Charleston was bristling with tension over a looming hospital strike that pitted underpaid black workers against the white administration. The strike brought national civil rights leaders to Charleston to denounce the firing of black nurses.

Finally, the tension erupted, resulting in burning buildings and hundreds of arrests. As a medical administrator, Dr. Colbert worked behind the scenes with civil rights leader Andrew Young to settle the strike. Decades later, when Dr. Colbert's youngest son had become a media sensation, Young went on *The Colbert Report* to discuss the strike. "What your father did was be reasonable and be humble," Young said. "He had good manners. He was a Southern gentleman from New York. That's very unusual."

Keeping a diplomatic distance from troubled Charleston, the Colberts moved into their own elegant home on James Island, just south of the city center. "James Island was like moving to the moon," Colbert remembered. "It was very sleepy, with dogs sleeping in the street. When I read *To Kill a Mockingbird*, I pictured the town where I grew up. It had dirt roads and some really ramshackle neighborhoods where the black people still lived, essentially in the houses where their ancestors had been slaves. And there were cotton fields and peanut fields and tomato sheds."

With five children off to college, the Colbert humorocracy was more manageable, but as a Catholic in a Protestant state, Stephen felt out of place. Once when he told a fellow first-grader of his faith, the boy said all Catholics were going to hell. His mother had told him so. Stephen also had health issues, including a tumor on his eardrum requiring surgery that left him deaf in his right ear. But instead of struggling to fit in, as most kids would have, Stephen remained true to his family heritage.

Dr. Colbert defied racial taboos, speaking openly in African-American churches while Stephen shunned all temptations to adopt a Southern accent. Television taught him that "Southern" amounted to "a shorthand that someone was stupid." America might have chuckled along with "*Hee-Haw*" and "*Green Acres*," but Colbert's television role models were news anchormen whose smooth speech he later mimicked.

Gradually, as Stephen advanced through grade school, the Colberts became accustomed to South

Carolina, his father buying a boat and sailing around Charleston Bay. Stephen was encouraged by both parents. "Even though my dad was a doctor, he was always saying, 'Go be a whaler. Be an ice climber. You don't want to be a lawyer; go raft the Amazon'. . . . The rule in our house was 'never refuse a legitimate adventure.'"

Colbert went fishing, played with friends, and dreamt of being almost anything but a comedian - a marine biologist, perhaps. Then, when he was ten, the Colberts suffered a life-altering tragedy.

On September 11, 1974, Colbert had just begun fourth grade. That morning before school, he hugged his father and two older brothers goodbye. Peter and Paul were off to boarding school in Connecticut, and Dr. Colbert was going along to get them settled. They never made it. Descending into Charlotte, North Carolina, in a thick fog, their plane skidded into a cornfield. Ten passengers survived to tell horrific stories of a flaming fuselage, bodies strewn about, and the frantic struggles to escape the wreckage.

Rescue teams scrambled, but as they approached the smoking plane, explosions tore it apart, killing the five dozen passengers trapped inside. Dr. Colbert and his two sons were among them. Investigating the crash, the National Traffic Safety Board blamed "poor cockpit discipline" and a crew that "did not follow prescribed procedure."

Stephen Colbert still mourns. "Grief," he said, "will always accept the invitation to appear. It's got plenty of time for you."

The list of comedians who have lost their fathers through death or divorce is a long one. It ranges from Lucille Ball to Mel Brooks, Lenny Bruce, Drew Carey, George Carlin, Charlie Chaplin, Louis C.K., Eddie Murphy, Richard Pryor, the Smothers Brothers, and Jon Stewart. What is there in tragedy that turns to humor: the need to cheer up a grieving mother; the need to cheer oneself; the drive to create a world where laughter trumps silence? Whatever the motive, ten-year-old Stephen Colbert did not find it at first. "Nothing made any sense after my father and my brothers died," Colbert said. "I kind of just shut off."

Colbert found his escape not in *MAD* magazine or television sitcoms but in books. Alone with his mother in a house where "the shades were down and she wore a lot of black," he read, on average, a book a day for eight years. He plowed through science fiction and fantasy, quickly finding favorites. In the *Chronicles of Thomas Covenant* series, he found his staunch Catholic faith tested but triumphant. In Fritz Leiber's *Lankhmar* series, he discovered swordsmanship and heroism. And when he could tear himself away from reading, he found a parallel world in the new role-playing game, Dungeons & Dragons, aka, D&D.

"I started playing Dungeons & Dragons the first week it was introduced to the market," Colbert recalled. Whether as Cleric or Druid, Paladin, Ranger, or some other D&D role, Colbert was "hooked." In 1977, when he and his mother moved from rustic James Island to the city of Charleston, Colbert felt even more of an outsider. Sent to the prestigious Porter-Gaud prep school, he clung to fantasy, reading book after book, rolling D&D's polyhedral dice, living life as a Dungeon Master. Did he do a lot of homework? "I put more effort into that game than I ever did into my schoolwork."

Absorbing hit points, performing feats, reveling in each revised version of the game, Colbert moved on into high school. There he discovered more literate fantasy in the works of J.R.R. Tolkien. Like many a lonely dreamer, Colbert saw Tolkien's Middle-earth not as a mere setting for a novel but a refuge. Gandalf and Frodo, Mordor and Gondor, and The Shire - he devoured *Lord of the Rings* again and again. Colbert estimates that he read the trilogy forty times. His office at Comedy Central, filled with Tolkien memorabilia, has been described as "a shrine to all things *Lord of the Rings*." In 2011, when director Peter Jackson invited Colbert to New Zealand to watch the filming of *The Hobbit*, Colbert took on Jackson and others in a Tolkien trivia contest. Colbert won.

Throughout his first two years of high school, Colbert was harassed and ostracized. Short, quiet, and nerdy, he was the perfect target for the once-and-future bullies who stalk every prep school. Then, in his junior year, as if assuming the role of a new character, Colbert blossomed. Perhaps all that fantasy was wearing thin, or maybe it was the young woman he had a crush on and for whom he wrote short vignettes describing the grisly deaths of her most-hated teacher. Or credit the comedy albums he played so often that he memorized them – Bill Cosby, George Carlin, Steve Martin. . . .

Whatever the reason, suddenly the short, quiet, nerdy Stephen Colbert became the most popular funnyman in his prep school. Joining the debate team and the glee club and winning the lead in school plays, he charmed teachers and students alike. He was, one teacher remembered, "brilliant, a little naughty, and supercharged with energy." He was, in short, the Stephen Colbert we see on TV today - minus the seasoning.

The seasoning began in college. Most of the Colberts attended the University of South Carolina, but Stephen's mediocre grades kept him out. Instead, he chose the ultra-conservative, all-male Hampden-Sydney College in Virginia. The oldest private college in the South, it was as stilted as its motto: "Come here as boys so you may leave as men." Hampden-Sydney's football team, fraternities, and nineteenth-century curriculum gave Colbert insight into the mainstream American values he now so sarcastically champions, but he hated his two years there.

"It was a 'playtime's over' kind of place," he recalled. Sullen and depressed, he lost fifty pounds and sank into "belated grieving." He found an outlet by acting in plays. One was the darkly-comic and oddly-titled, *Oh Dad, Poor Dad, Mamma's Hung You in the Closet and I'm Feelin' So Sad.* Colbert remembered thinking, "This is for me - dark farce."

Serious about acting, he even did a nude scene at the Spoleto Festival. At the request of Ken Russell, the controversial director of *Women in Love* and other films, he stood alone on stage naked in Puccini's *Madama Butterfly.* Someone so dedicated to acting did not belong at a strict, southern men's college. So, as he approached his junior year, Colbert began looking for theater schools. Among the best, he learned, was Northwestern University in Evanston, Illinois. Colbert applied and was accepted.

Like Hampden-Sydney, Northwestern had football and fraternities, but it was also just a short "L" train ride from Chicago where a young wit could watch seasoned pros stretch themselves on the rack of comedy improvisation. Though he came north to become a dramatic actor, it would be in improv's fantasy world - lightning fast, unpredictable, and as combative as anything out of Tolkien - that the southern Catholic Stephen Colbert would make his name. And that name would differ from the family moniker.

On the plane to Chicago, Colbert decided to soften his surname. Bumped up to first class, he struck up a conversation with his seatmate, an astronaut. He told the man he was on his way to a new school, a new life. "Oh, wow!" the astronaut said, "you could really reinvent yourself out there."

"When the plane took off I was Colbert," Stephen recalled, "and when the plane landed, I was Colbear." Forever after, the "t" would be silent, but it would take years before the man who made it that way learned to speak from his gut.

CHAPTER 2
HIGH-STATUS FOOL

"Attack life, it's going to kill you anyway."

Every member of Colbert Nation has a favorite interview. There was the time Colbert flattered Bill O'Reilly of Fox News by telling him, "I'm living your book," then held up a copy with a discount sticker over O'Reilly's face. Then there was the time Colbert puzzled children's author Maurice Sendak by suggesting a sequel to *Where the Wild Things Are*. Subtitled *Still Wilding*, the book would star Vin Diesel, with tie-ins to Burger King or Taco Bell. And then there was the time Colbert challenged rock-star Jack White to a "Catholic Throwdown" in which the two stumbled through hymns, debated dogma, and posed "gotcha" questions about obscure saints.

COLBERT: "Who's the patron saint of ummm . . . clowns?"

WHITE: "Who's the patron saint of clowns? Maybe Saint Joseph?"

COLBERT: "St. Genesius!"

WHITE: "Really? I don't think that's a real saint."

Most news/talk shows use interviews as a tired, but time-tested ritual: Don't have much to say? Get a guest without much to say. But in Colbert's hands, interviews are adventures, and may St. Genesius - who is, in fact, the Catholic patron saint of clowns - help any guest who walks blindly into a Stephen Colbert interview. One of the first was Democratic Congressman Robert Wexler in 2006. Proudly representing Florida's 19th District in *The Colbert Report* segment, "Better Know a District," Wexler began by boasting about his constituents. He looked forward to softball questions, but Colbert became Colbert. First, he suggested drilling for oil off the coast of Florida. When Wexler rejected that idea, Colbert asked whether he supported drilling in Alaska.

WEXLER: "No."

COLBERT: "So caribou are more important than my SUV?"

WEXLER: "No, no. . . ."

COLBERT: "But that's what you just said."

WEXLER: "What's most important is that your SUV be required to have better efficiency in the future."

COLBERT: "What if I could make it run on caribou meat? Would you be in favor of that?"

WEXLER: "On caribou meat?"

COLBERT: "Caribou meat. Or hide, doesn't matter. Or bone."

WEXLER: "Probably not."

COLBERT: "Why?"

WEXLER: "Because we'd have to kill all the caribou to get you to drive your SUV."

COLBERT: "So caribou are more important than my SUV."

WEXLER: "No, I think we can have both...."

COLBERT: "So why can't I kill them and grind them up and put them in my SUV?"

WEXLER: "Because I think we can have both caribou and SUVS that get better gas mileage."

COLBERT: "Let's move on here...."

Moving on, Colbert asked the congressman to complete the sentences: "I enjoy cocaine because. . . ." and "I enjoy the company of prostitutes for the following reasons. . . ."

Politicians and professors, rock stars and renowned experts, Colbert has out-dueled them all. His innate intelligence is one reason, but Colbert learned to wing it in the best possible schools – Chicago stages.

Improvisational comedy, the art of turning a single audience suggestion into a full-fledged skit on the fly, made its American debut in Chicago. In the late 1940s, drama teacher Viola Spolin began giving young actors a series of "theater games" that demanded quickness and a stifling of the internal monitor that keeps most of us quiet. "Shut off the mind," Spolin taught. "When the rational mind is shut off, we have the possibility of intuition." The trick to improv, she maintained, is "to get out of the head." The trick went on stage in 1959 when Spolin's son, Paul Sills, opened a small nightclub in Chicago's Old Town neighborhood. The club was called the Second City, and it heralded a new type of American comedy.

Before Second City, comedy remained in the shadow of vaudeville and radio. On TV, aging vaudevillians such as George Burns, Bob Hope, and Red Skelton turned up on show after show, and sitcoms like *Ozzie and Harriet, Our Miss Brooks,* and *The Jack Benny Show* were nothing more than old radio serials performed before the cameras. Second City changed all that. To its small stage came the wits who would take American comedy into the age of *Saturday Night Live*. Their names are still legendary in comedic circles - Mike Nichols and Elaine May, Alan Arkin, Joan Rivers, David Steinberg, and Robert Klein. Then came the next generation, some from a Second City spin-off in Toronto - John Belushi, Dan Aykroyd, Gilda Radner, Bill Murray, and Martin Short.

By 1984, when Colbert transferred to Northwestern, Second City's legacy on *Saturday Night Live* was widely known. Colbert, however, had little time for comedy. He may have been witty back in South Carolina, but in Chicago he would be – an actor. In drama classes at Northwestern, he was known not for his humor but his intensity and occasional rage. One professor, frightened by his anger in a scene, suggested he seek therapy. In another instance, Colbert nearly broke an actor's hand during a rehearsal. "I had a short fuse back then," he remembers. "I was a real poet-slash-jerk."

Northwestern, a Big Ten university on the windy shores of Lake Michigan, subjected the young man from South Carolina to a series of culture shocks. Raised a prim and proper Catholic, Colbert was now living in a coed dorm, meeting openly gay students and suffering through long, frigid winters. "Minus 70 wind chill," he recalled. "Minus

39 regular one night." Colbert defended himself with attitude - growing a beard, wearing black turtlenecks, replacing his slow, Southern demeanor with a crisp, academic gravity. Yet he also worked tirelessly, waiting tables, acting in dramas, studying ballet and method acting, and completing a three-year curriculum in just two.

One night during Colbert's junior year, a friend took him to an improv theater in downtown Chicago. Though it was not Second City, the show opened Colbert to the adventure of improv. He considered Second City "a little cult," so he decided to form his own improv troupe at Northwestern. Made up not just of theater majors, but also engineering and math students, too, the "No Fun Mud Piranhas" had plenty of fun, even competing in a nationwide improv competition. Yale won, but Colbert became still more serious about improv. He began studying with Del Close, a celebrated teacher at Chicago's ImprovOlympic. Known for his temper and fierce devotion to his art, Close taught Colbert to "jump down the rabbit hole." In other words, let the skit unfold, Colbert recalled, while "being willing to surrender what your plan was for the discovery of the moment."

While other comedians abandoned the characters they had played as class clowns, Colbert took an alternate route. He drew on his vast reading and the lessons learned in his intellectual family. "The smarter you are, the better you're going to be at this work," said Charna Halpern, one of Colbert's first improv teachers. "Stephen was so aware of the world around him that he could talk about anything."

When Colbert graduated in 1986, he watched fellow theater grads head for New York or Los Angeles. But now torn between improv and dramatic acting, he chose to stay in Chicago. He still scorned Second City, considering its polished skits less than pure forms of the art, but after a year of waiting tables, tending bar, and auditioning for stage roles he did not get, Colbert became less particular. He began to question his goal of becoming a serious actor. When he blew a line in *Hamlet*, fellow actors were icy, but when he blew a line in a skit, everyone laughed anyway.

A job building furniture offered no future, and a soul-searching swing through Europe just made him lonely. Finally, in 1987, broke, discouraged, sleeping on a friend's floor, he jumped at the chance to work in the Second City box office. The work was menial, but it had one significant perk - free improv classes. Colbert was soon living in a loft, selling tickets, and learning to "get out of the head." He survived another Chicago winter, and in August 1988, his hard work and intelligent wit earned him a place in the Second City touring company.

Second City thrives on zaniness. Each of its revues, though given one clever title, is a montage of quick sketches, with the audience asked to focus attention stage left, right, or center. Two or three players act out sketches lasting two or three minutes before the action shifts again. Second City can be equally frenetic offstage, where performers can "get out of the head" in more ways than one. Drugs and alcohol are no strangers to the company. Where, in a motley crew of overgrown boys and girls, would a socially conservative son of the South fit?

Colbert enjoyed Second City. "I liked the fact that a lot of people who worked there were sort of damaged," he said, but would its audiences enjoy Colbert? At first, he confined his roles to "high-status fools," tight-lipped, moralistic men who were "shocked, shocked" at the antics going on around them. A Polaroid photo of Colbert taken at the Second City Training Center shows how perfectly he fit the part. While others training with him were sassy (Amy Sedaris) or sloppy (Chris Farley), the Polaroid of Colbert captures him in striped shirt and dark tie, clean-cut, sober, more likely to be hired by a bank than an improv troupe. Fellow Second City hires instantly recognized his intelligence, but would he ever loosen up?

"I was very 'actorly' because I had gone to theater school," Colbert admitted. "And I was very controlled. I was all about planning." Fellow comics soon decided to take Colbert down a notch. His boast that he had never broken up onstage was an irresistible challenge. It wasn't long before Amy Sedaris took the challenge.

Amy, younger sister of the author David Sedaris, was just beginning her career. Though she was lovely enough to be a Hollywood star, the offbeat humor she shared with her brother inspired characters she created with wigs and gaudy makeup. Hearing Colbert's boast of his onstage composure, Sedaris vowed to make him lose it. When a song the two were singing called for her to smile, she revealed a set of hideous false teeth. Colbert cracked up, managed to finish the song, then ran backstage to crack up in a different way.

"I fucking blew offstage and went and locked myself in the bathroom like a teenage girl and banged my head against the wall with rage." Sedaris and another troupe member, Paul Dinello, heard the banging and stood at the door, shouting, "Hey, you cryin'?" The mocking continued for a few minutes. When he emerged, embarrassed but composed, Colbert saw that anger worked better as an act than as a lifestyle. "They completely won," he said. "I'm forever grateful that they broke me."

From that evening on, Colbert, Sedaris, and Dinello were inseparable. The working-class Dinello and the courtly Colbert overcame initial resentments and with the help of the wacky Sedaris teamed up to create wilder and wilder skits. "They were the magic trio," said Second City veteran Dave Razowski. Dinello and Sedaris were a couple, but they did not mind Colbert tagging along. And whenever Colbert got too serious - he was still auditioning for dramatic roles - Sedaris and Dinello talked him back into comedy. Sedaris was Colbert's female foil, and Dinello was the anti-Colbert. Raised in gritty Chicago, he projected a brash stupidity that contrasted with Colbert's prim fools. By 1990, calling themselves "The Three Idiots," Colbert, Dinello, and Sedaris had improvised their way from Second City's touring troupe to Second City e.t.c., a branch theater in northwest Chicago. It was still not the main stage in Old Town, but they were getting close.

As he grew more confident, Colbert also became more social. Since his blossoming in prep school junior year, he had been a jokester around women but rarely a suitor. He met no women at all-male Hampden-Sydney and was too busy to date much at Northwestern. Only when he started taking classes at Second City did he begin to take the opposite sex seriously. After going out with several women, he stayed with one until she demanded a deeper commitment. During the spring of 1990, he flew to Charleston to talk to his mother about this ultimatum. While there, he went to an opera at the historic Dock Street Theater in the antebellum heart of the city. During intermission, he spotted *her*.

The lobby of the theater is Charleston's finest, with plush carpet, colonial staircases, and a posh crowd in gowns and tuxes. But even among such elegance, one woman caught Colbert's attention. "I walk in, and I see this woman across the lobby and I thought, 'That one. Right there.'" He told himself he was crazy, but he strode across the lobby and introduced himself. They had much in common. Evelyn McGee, like Colbert, was from a distinguished Charleston family. Her father was a prominent lawyer in the city and had served in the state's House of Representatives. Evelyn had gone to prep school, enjoyed theater, had done some acting, and was a fan of the poet E.E. Cummings.

Perhaps Colbert impressed her by mentioning that he had appeared in a Chicago production of Cummings' memoir, *The Enormous Room*. Perhaps he did not need to impress her that way. She may have already sensed how kind and generous he is, how smart he is. The two talked throughout intermission, met again after the opera, and when Colbert returned to Chicago, they began a long-distance courtship. In those days, that meant letters and late-night phone calls. Luckily, Colbert was up late, thanks to his job.

Second City thrives on teamwork, its actors following one of Viola Spolin's principles to "always agree, always go along" with a skit as it unfolds. The phrase Second City lives by is, "yes, and. . . ." Once welcomed to the troupe's stage, Colbert found it easy to say "yes." His penchant for playing straight-laced fools was a good fit with the team, earning him roles in *Ku Klux Klambake, Destiny, and How to Avoid It,* and *Where's Your God Now, Charlie Brown?*

By 1991, however, Second City's reputation had become a handicap. How could the troupe that spawned Nichols and May, Belushi and Aykroyd, Martin Short and now Mike Myers be as funny as it once was? Chicago critics had tired of the troupe. Second City, the *Chicago Reader* wrote, "is not in business to change the world; it's here to sell drinks, give the audience a couple of chuckles, and send them home with a smile and a good buzz." But even the staunchest critics had to admit that every Second City show had its moments. Colbert provided one when he dreamed up a black woman as his alter ego.

By 1992, Colbert had moved from Second City e.t.c. to its main stage in Old Town Chicago. His first job there was as understudy to Steve Carell, who would later star with him on *The Daily Show* before going on to *The Office*. Carell, like Colbert, had grown up in a prim Catholic family and was getting laughs by acting clueless. In early 1993, after watching poet Maya Angelou read at President Bill Clinton's inauguration, Colbert began thinking, "I wish I was an old black woman! They have so much character."

With that inspiration, Colbert and Carell crafted a sketch where the two of them were heading back to their southern hometowns. The sketch had them riding a train, discussing how great it was to be back home, waxing nostalgic until they stepped onto the platform. A woman then approached Colbert, calling him Shirley Wentworth. Reviving his southern accent, he responded in kind, spewing phrases like, "Oh, honey, I'm sorry to hear that," and "I love you, too, darlin.'" Turning to Carell, Colbert said, "I forgot to tell you. When I'm home, I'm an old black woman."

With fresh talent, the new Second City won over critics. The *Chicago Reader* praised the latest revue as "[f]ree of boneheaded skits and blessed with some dramatic and comic inspiration and swift interplay between the unmellow seven cast members." The *Reader* singled out Colbert as "effortlessly arrogant."

His career solidifying, Colbert continued his long-distance courtship of Evelyn McGee. He sent letters containing love poems by E.E. Cummings. Their calls lasted longer into the night, but the couple had seen each other only when Colbert went to Charleston for Christmas and on occasional trysts in New York, where Evelyn was living. Once, when a Second City sketch required Colbert to learn a few notes on the trombone, he showed up outside Evelyn's Manhattan flat to offer a brass serenade.

By the summer of 1993, however, the distance between them required closing.

They talked, then agreed. Evelyn moved to Chicago, where she took a job as the development director for an avant-garde theater company. Before long, Stephen and Evie, as she was known, were living together in Chicago's Lincoln Park neighborhood. And on October 9, 1993, the Second City's revue had an understudy playing many of its key roles. That afternoon, in the Second Presbyterian Church of Charleston, South Carolina, Stephen Tyrone Colbert and Evelyn Brabham McGee married. After their honeymoon, the Colberts returned to Chicago, but they were already making other plans.

Colbert had ridden live, sketch comedy as far as Second City could take him. "I was there for five years," he said, "and it was everything to me." But having seen other Second City stars rise still higher, he hoped to follow in their footsteps. Perhaps he would try television like the *Saturday Night Live* legends, or even movies. Ten years had passed since Colbert arrived in the Chicago area as an effete, twenty-year-old Southerner who had just fine-tuned his last name. He had been prim, proper, angry, lonely - "really willing to share my grief with you," he said. In 1994, he left Chicago as a seasoned comic, relaxed, inventive, and lightning quick. What might America's first city, New York, offer a "high-status fool?"

CHAPTER 3
WINGING IT

*"There's no status I would not surrender
for a joke."*

The camera opens on a beat-up old car rolling along a wooded interstate. The driver is listening to radio bulletins. It seems that a serial killer is on the loose, leaving various body parts in his wake. The suspect is a white male, middle-aged, 180 pounds – in short, identical to the car's driver. Up ahead, he sees five hitchhikers. He pulls over. All five pile into the backseat. As the car roars back onto the highway, a bubbly theme song starts: "If I Knew You Were Comin' I'd of Baked a Cake."

Rolling down the road, the hitchhikers exchange suspicious glances. It appears that the dog in the front seat has fake fangs. There's a rattlesnake in the car. The driver is snuffing out cigarettes on his bald spot. Now he's taking Polaroid pictures of the stars, each shown as a still above the names Paul

Dinello, Amy Sedaris, Stephen Colbert. When the car pulls off at Exit 57, the show has its title but not its audience.

Every class has its clown and every party its "life of." Yet local wits who take their humor to bigger stages can choose from just two paths, sketch comedy or stand-up. Back when Colbert was playing Dungeons & Dragons, odds favored the sketch comedian. Stand-up was in retreat, holding its shrinking audience by being brash or outlandish like George Carlin, Steve Martin, and Richard Pryor. Sketch comedy, meanwhile, had taken off with the 1975 debut of *Saturday Night Live*, which spawned *ABC's Fridays* and endless re-runs of *Monty Python's Flying Circus*. By 1984, when Colbert arrived in Chicago, the biggest comic roles in movies and TV were going to former sketch comedians Dan Aykroyd, Chevy Chase, Bill Murray, and the like. But then the stage shifted.

During the years Colbert was learning to be professionally funny, stand-up comedy cleaned up its act and rose from the dead. Throughout the 1980s, more than 300 comedy clubs opened across the United States. Beyond Greenwich Village's legendary The Bitter End, stand-ups were getting laughs in Memphis, Tennessee; San Antonio, Texas; San Diego, California; Omaha, Nebraska; and points in between. Stand-up became a regular feature of cable TV, and any star said to be rising was going it alone. One charismatic comic was all it took to make a hit TV show or movie, so by the time Colbert moved to New York in 1994, the biggest comic roles were being snatched up by former stand-ups – Tim Allen, Roseanne Barr, Ray Romano, Chris Rock, and Jerry Seinfeld. Colbert, who had never shown the slightest interest in stand-up, was in for some lean years.

But Stephen did not come to New York solely with his new wife. Amy Sedaris and Paul Dinello, though no longer a couple, moved to New York to try sketch comedy off-Broadway. Accompanying them was Amy's brother, David, who had just published *Barrel Fever,* his debut book of bizarrely funny stories. David had also written his first play, *Stitches,* the story of a disfigured woman given her own TV show, which leads to a nation of fans disfiguring their own faces.

HBO execs loved the quirky play and hired two of its stars, Paul and Amy, to write a pilot for a sketch comedy show. They, in turn, called Colbert in Chicago to see if he would help. On this thin hope, Stephen and Evie packed and moved to New York. "The Three Idiots" were reunited. Pleased with the pilot, HBO ordered six half-hour episodes as a trial run. "They left us alone for four months at a time to write," Colbert remembered. "We had a lot of freedom." In the winter of 1995, *Exit 57* debuted.

Following its serial-killer opening, *Exit 57* was brought to prime time. "The Three Idiots" hoped the show might be the next *SNL*, but it lacked the filter of Lorne Michaels, the savvy *SNL* producer who knew precisely what was not ready for prime time. Colbert and company soon learned that comedy on a small stage seems even smaller on a studio set.

Performing before a live audience instead of using a laugh track, gag after gag played to smatterings of chuckles. Each skit was set in the Midwestern town of Quad Cities, a spin-off from David Lynch's cultish series, *Twin Peaks*. Many of the gags were funny, some very funny. There was Colbert as a smooth-talker who shows his date a porn video, records her outrage, and plays it back to himself after she storms out. Then there was Colbert as dutiful father, asking Dinello whether he "got any tonight" with his daughter. When Dinello says "no," Colbert sits beside him. "Pretend I'm her," he says, and the two kiss. And there was "Trudy and Eddy - The White Trash Couple," with Colbert and Sedaris as marriage counselors undressing in front of clients, and Colbert as a surgeon juggling body parts.

"No one can really figure it out," Dinello told the *Chicago Sun-Times*. "We never sat down and said this is our concept." Colbert said simply, "We try to amuse ourselves." It was hard to tell how many others were amused by *Exit 57*, but the show certainly confused critics. *The New York Times* derided its "off-kilter" tone while *Rolling Stone* liked the show: "Although some bits play more like darkly funny one-acts than sketches, others can vault you into the comic stratosphere once reserved for *SNL.*" Ratings were equally mixed. Early numbers were high enough to earn *Exit 57* another six shows in September 1995, and the show was nominated for CableACE awards in the categories of best writing and best comedy series. But audiences quickly turned away, and the ride ended after a dozen episodes. So forgettable was *Exit 57* that even now, with Colbert one of TV's biggest stars, old segments on YouTube have just a few thousand hits.

By the time *Exit 57* was canceled, Stephen and Evie were the parents of Madeleine Colbert, named for Evie's mother. Colbert, with his wife choosing to be a stay-at-home mom, now had more pressure to be professionally funny. The thirty-one-year-old father took his high-status foolishness back to the audition circuit, where he was turned down repeatedly. With so many stand-up comics around, TV execs no longer needed the Second City veterans.

"I was completely desperate," Colbert remembered. He even resorted to using infant Madeleine as a puppet in an audition tape. That tape got him a job as a writer and performer on the one last bastion of sketch comedy, *The Dana Carvey Show.*

Carvey's eerily accurate impressions had made him a standout on *SNL,* and his goofy Garth character turned the phrase "NOT!" into a cultural staple in the movie, *Wayne's World.* Working with Carvey, Colbert looked forward to years of steady employment. How could such a talent, bolstered by Colbert, Steve Carell, and *SNL* writer Robert Smigel go the way of *Exit 57*?

Timing is everything in comedy. Anyone can get a laugh at a dull party, in a boring classroom, or around an office water cooler. But the ability to pause just long enough, then deliver a punch line or a pratfall is the skill young actors line up to learn. And in a cultural context, timing can determine the fate of entire shows. *SNL,* so fresh in 1975, seemed stale a decade later. Watch a clip of *Rowan and Martin's Laugh-in* and see if it amuses. *The Dana Carvey Show,* by contrast, still seems funny, and Colbert and Carell are two reasons why.

In "Waiters Who Are Nauseated By Food," they read menu specials to diners while trying not to retch. "Leftover Beatle Memories" played off the then-recent *Beatles Anthology* documentary. Carvey played a bouncy Paul, Smigel a snoring Ringo, and Colbert a mustachioed George with a Liverpudlian accent: "I killed a man once. I think it was a stagehand. He looked at me funny, so I had to. It was all taken care of by the record company, so no one found out."

But other bits seemed poorly timed. Was America ready for a President Clinton nursing baby animals from plastic breasts? And was Taco Bell, the show's sponsor, ready for a dancing taco presenting Carvey with a big check, and calling him a "shameless whore?" Apparently it was not: Taco Bell pulled out after two shows. Just seven more aired, and Colbert was unemployed again. Today, *The Dana Carvey Show* is seen as having been ahead of its time, and it is credited with boosting the careers of Colbert, Carell, Louis C.K., and the screenwriter of *Being John Malkovich,* Charlie Kaufman. But Carvey later called it "probably the most bizarre variety show in the history of American television." Apparently, he missed the various shows hosted by Sonny and Cher.

Then came what Colbert called "the year where I wasn't doing anything." The crash of the Carvey show killed TV sketch comedy. America in the mid-nineties was in no mood for cynics. The economy was booming, the president was popular, and a dazzling parade of digital technology was changing entertainment, leisure, and life itself. The relative "good times" of the Clinton years spawned bland comedy. Viewers were happy with *Friends*, the *Single Guy*, and *Home Improvement*. At the box office, comedies were safe and retrograde – *101 Dalmatians*, *The Nutty Professor*, and the latest Jim Carrey vehicle featuring another Jerry Lewis shtick. Colbert, stuck in New York with a wife and child, grabbed any gig he could get.

In his year of "not doing anything," Colbert: helped Robert Smigel turn the Carvey show into an animated superhero spoof, *The Ambiguously Gay Duo*, that found a home on *SNL*; contracted with *Good Morning, America* to do short humorous pieces; (He pitched twenty but shot just one, a straight-faced visit to a Rube Goldberg design competition.) did a voice-over on *The Chris Rock Show*; got a cameo on the Michael J. Fox sitcom, *Spin City*; did a commercial for a Nebraska bank; and landed a humor piece on the Op-Ed page of *The New York Times*.

The *Times*' piece played off news of a rocket car that had set a land speed record of 763 miles per hour. Colbert and Paul Dinello speculated on a future with "a rocket car in every driveway!" Milk deliveries, ambulance runs, and paper routes would be made - all at top speeds of 700 miles per hour, but only if the government provided the infrastructure. "Clearly, the future belongs to the long, flat, sandy straightaway. . . . And once we've paved the oceans, there will be no stopping us."

Selling himself as never before, Colbert went to plenty of auditions but landed no permanent gigs. With his wife at home and his daughter beginning to toddle, "I thought I made a huge mistake in what I decided to do for a living." He saw little chance of starting over. "It wasn't like I was going to go to law school. It was too late. The die was cast."

Colbert's older siblings had carried on their father's professionalism, becoming lawyers, executives, and trade specialists. But young Stephen Colbert was on the verge of becoming just another Second City veteran who aimed to be the next Belushi but went off to New York and disappeared. His demeanor could have allowed him to become a TV anchorman in some mid-level city, or he could have ended up as the funniest father at kids' birthday parties. He might have been an amazing used-car salesman. All three seemed more likely than the remote chance that this hybrid of the straight-laced South and Chicago improv stages would become the most celebrated wit in America.

But deep in the blandness of Clinton nation, the seeds of Colbert Nation had been sown. On July 22, 1996, Comedy Central debuted its late-night entry, *The Daily Show*. Given its current eminence – eighteen Emmys and counting – *The Daily Show* of 1996-98 should be called, *The Daily Show Without Jon Stewart*. Host Craig Kilborn, a veteran of ESPN Sports Center, did his best with modest news parodies, celebrity guests, and the occasional bright spot such as "This Week in God" or "Your Moment of Zen."

Reports from the show's correspondents were "News of the Weird" accounts: stories about Bigfoot, aliens, or animals doing things that animals look ridiculous doing. Kilborn enjoyed embarrassing his guests by asking "The Five Questions." Based on questions the handsome host asked his dates, they included: "Canada: What Went Wrong?"; "Who Left the Cake Out in the Rain?"; and "Spell 'Monogamy.'" This early version of the show drew a half-million viewers, acceptable by late-night standards but dismissed by critics as trivial and mean-spirited.

Colbert never watched it, yet in the spring of 1997 when his agent got him an audition to become a correspondent, he had little choice but to show up. *The Daily Show* producer, Madeline Smithberg, had seen "Waiters Who Are Nauseated by Food," and it "just cracked me up," she said. So when Colbert auditioned by pitching stories that *Good Morning, America* had turned down, he was signed to a contract. He was less than thrilled. "It was totally a day job. I did not believe in the show, I did not watch the show, and they paid dirt. It was literally just a paycheck to show up."

To Colbert's surprise, *The Daily Show* correspondents were expected to do more than read on camera. Each had to seek out weird stories, travel to the scene, write a script, and shoot footage in one or two takes. Doing 120 pieces a year was hard for a sketch master accustomed to polishing and perfecting each gag, but Colbert's ability to wing it paid off. And his early years of mimicking TV newsmen made him ideally suited to fake news.

Both Groucho Marx and French diplomat Jean Giraudoux have been credited with saying that the key to success is sincerity: "Once you can fake that, you've got it made." In developing his *Daily Show* persona, Colbert took the adage a step further. Nodding, pausing, then drilling the camera with his gaze, he seemed professional and so, so sincere. Yet once the viewer saw that he was covering another Bigfoot story, sincerity became the joke. Moving further into the piece, Colbert amped up the gravitas, dipping an eyebrow, adjusting his glasses to become the dead-on parody of a news correspondent - Geraldo Rivera without pants. Anderson Cooper on Red Bull.

It took Colbert a while to warm to *The Daily Show* and vice versa. Tensions on the set were high as host Kilborn joked about the "bitches" behind the scenes, and no one on either side of the camera seemed sure when fakeness was funny or when it was just fake. Colbert appreciated the steady pay but later lamented, "You wanted to take your soul off, put it on a wire hanger, and leave it in the closet before you got on the plane to do one of these pieces." Not expecting the show to last, he continued to seek other work but came up empty. Then, in December 1998, as he and Evie celebrated the birth of their son Peter, "The Three Idiots" struck again.

As children of the 1970s, all three remembered watching smarmy after-school specials about troubled teens. All that angst begged for mockery, and Colbert, Dinello, and Sedaris were ready to take aim. They pitched a pilot to Comedy Central, entitled *The Way After School Special*, that portrayed Amy Sedaris as a former "user, boozer, and loser" who returns to high school as a creepy, clueless, middle-aged woman. Faculty at the fictional Flatpoint High consisted of angry, hair-triggered teachers, screaming or bursting into tears in front of their classes. Comedy Central bought ten episodes and gave the show the best slot on the network, right after *South Park*. Colbert, Dinello, and Sedaris got busy writing.

A month after they sold the idea, a new host appeared on *The Daily Show*. Together with Colbert, he would pave a third path for young comics - satire.

CHAPTER 4
AMERICA'S ANCHORS

"I tried to be like Jon Stewart, and by trying to be him, I found myself."

On a warm mid-August day in 1998, while Americans reveled in the latest dirt from the Clinton-Lewinsky scandal, Comedy Central held a press conference in Manhattan. Beneath the network's globe-shaped logo, executives told reporters of a forthcoming change at the anchor desk of *The Daily Show*. Host Craig Kilborn was jumping to the CBS *Late Late Show*, leaving Comedy Central moguls miffed. Like jilted lovers, they did not want to talk about it. How could they possibly replace Kilborn?

In answer, their new host stepped to the podium.

He was short, as he was quick to note, nearly a foot shorter than Kilborn. He was also handsome, affable, and eager to take the tired show in a fresh direction. Younger reporters may have recognized him from his MTV late night show, canceled four years earlier. Since then, he had struggled to stay afloat, taking bit parts in movies, guest hosting, and continuing to do stand-up. Ladies and gentlemen, meet Jon Stewart.

Responding to questions, Stewart dismissed the change as "musical chairs," but when pressed, he promised changes. "When you go into a show, you want to establish your own identity," he said. Another reporter raised his hand. Aside from the steady income, why had Stewart, often rumored to be courted by major networks, signed onto cable? "I value my anonymity," he quipped. Then came a question from the back. The reporter identified himself. "Stephen Colbert, Mr. Stewart. What I want to know is how does this announcement affect *my* chances of becoming host of *The Daily Show*?" Stewart turned to his new boss and said, "I thought you said he wasn't funny."

Later that day, Colbert told his wife about the new host of *The Daily Show*. It turned out she knew him. Back in the early 1990s, when Colbert was courting Evie long distance, her roommate was dating Stewart. Evie had often seen the young comedian sitting alone at parties, nursing a beer. "Jon Stewart?" she said incredulously. "He's not funny."

That evening, Colbert went to a Manhattan bookstore where Stewart was signing his book, *Naked Pictures of Famous People.* Chances are, no one noticed when the two men stood face-to-face at the book table. Stewart wrote: "To Stephen, Please don't hurt me - Jon Stewart." And as Stewart later said, "After that, it was all magic."

They were an unlikely couple. Aside from losing their fathers at age ten - Stewart in a bitter divorce, Colbert in a tragic plane crash - they had little in common. One was a wise-cracking New Jersey kid raised, along with his older brother, by a public school teacher. The other came from a huge and distinguished family ensconced in the upper echelons of Southern society. One grew up reading *MAD* magazine, the other devouring Tolkien. One was Jewish, the other Catholic. One did stand-up, the other sketch comedy. One was a thirty-five-year-old bachelor living with his girlfriend in lower Manhattan, the other a married father of a growing family and living in New York's tony Westchester County. One spiced his humor with words you couldn't say on television, the other relied on nuance and parody.

The man who would come to know them best, writer and producer Ben Karlin, later marveled at the contrast. "Stephen is a happy man," Karlin said. "He goes home to a lovely wife in New Jersey (the Colberts moved from New York in 2000), with a new dog and three beautiful children. He teaches Sunday school and knows his way around the kitchen. And then he has this deviously brilliant comedic mind. . . . Jon is driven by the forces of guilt and shame and fear of being on the outside that gives Jews their comic angst." But Stewart and Colbert, Karlin added, share one important trait. "They both really just want to get a laugh."

Until that press conference on August 11, 1998, Stewart and Colbert had never met and seemed barely aware of each other. Too old to watch MTV, Colbert had not seen *The Jon Stewart Show* that aired in the early '90s. Stewart may have watched *Exit 57*, but never having visited Second City, he was unaware of Colbert's improv background. Stewart was intensely political; Colbert avoided politics. But over the next several years, Jon Stewart and Stephen Colbert would merge their respective geniuses to become the most revered comic voices in America.

The hyphenated name, "Stewart-Colbert," now saturated American culture as if they were married. Every four years, it emerged on bumper stickers and T-shirts touting them for president and vice president. (In 2014, there was already a Stewart/Colbert 2016 Facebook page.) The duo routinely appeared in gossip columns and news bites summarizing what each said on his most recent show, and pundits have written about the

"Stewart-Colbert effect" on TV news. In the fall of 2010, they co-hosted the massive "Rally to Restore Sanity and/or Fear" on the National Mall in Washington, D.C. Barely more than a year later, they lampooned the entire election process by co-coordinating Colbert's Super PAC. Working independently, yet in lockstep, Jon Stewart and Stephen Colbert had become, as *"Rolling Stone"* magazine put it, "America's Anchors."

They were anchors in more ways than one. Each anchored fake news programs; each was also an anchor in a culture that seems increasingly insane. Their co-anchor work began on January 11, 1999, when Stewart took over *The Daily Show*. "Welcome to *The Daily Show!*" Stewart began. "Craig Kilborn is on assignment in Kuala Lumpur – I'm Jon Stewart." Then, after reading the usual fake headlines, he turned to the show's chief political correspondent, Colbert, standing before a backdrop of the U.S. Capitol.

Colbert detailed the merchandising surrounding the impending impeachment trial of President Clinton: T-shirts, snow globes, corn holders - all manner of products designed to capitalize on the furor. Chili's "El Diablo" was the Democrats' official fajita of the impeachment process, while the GOP was sponsored by "Lying Vindictive Hypocrites." The segment lasted just two minutes, but it was the beginning of a beautiful friendship.

Years later, Colbert waxed nostalgic about those early days, joking about how tightly he and Stewart are linked. "We live together, you know," Colbert told Jimmy Kimmel. "We commute to work on a tandem bicycle." But seriously, though, "I am so lucky to have Jon Stewart, of all people, call me up on a random day and say, 'I like that thing you did last night, and here's why. . . .' And he's also just a good, fun guy. I'm lucky to have him as a friend, and as a mentor."

Throughout Stewart's first year behind *The Daily Show* desk, Colbert continued to hone his deadpan character. As the show's correspondent, Colbert was not the grandiose, right-wing egotist who would later lead Colbert Nation. Instead, he was that fool's father. Grim, weighty, and melodramatic, he applied fake sincerity to one strange story after another. Masterful timing enabled Colbert to make even silence funny. The raw rookie, Stewart, could barely contain a smile when introducing the next Colbert segment. In a typical piece, Colbert traveled to Saratoga Springs, New York, "a safe, picturesque community, in reality, but on paper, it's home to one of the most deadly accidents of our time." Colbert then explained how 350 residents had been listed as "deceased" on W-2 forms.

"It was a misalignment in the printer," said a reporter, his face darkened.

"How many people died?" Colbert asked.

"No one died."

"Then why the 'x' under 'deceased?'"

"The printer made a mistake."

"And that ended up killing people?"

Insisting there had been a mass murder, he interrogated city officials:

"Is there rage?" he somberly asked. "Rage?" He also posed painful questions to the "deceased" seated before him. "All right, so nobody's dead, but does anyone have anything wrong . . . anything at all?" Silence. Finally, one man said, "My knee hurts."

"We only have a minute more," Colbert concluded. "Does anyone want to cry? We could use some tears."

Later, Colbert wrapped up the ongoing Bigfoot series, reporting from central Washington State where Sasquatch had made the Endangered Species List. And on the Wall Street trading floors, Senior Financial Correspondent Stephen Colbert discussed the World Wrestling Federation's new stock offering. Breaking into a testosterone-fed Hulk Hogan voice, he shouted: "YOU WANNA KNOW WHY THE YEN IS DOWN, YAMAMOTO? BECAUSE YOU PANTYWAISTS CAN'T HANDLE A GOLD-BACKED CURRENCY! THE NIKKEI [INDEX] IS FOR OLD LADIES AND BEDWETTERS!"

Feeling more in tune with Stewart than with Craig Kilborn, Colbert put his own stamp on *The Daily Show*. When other correspondents left, he was quick to recommend his old Second City foil, Steve Carell. "There's nothing he can't make funny," Colbert told the *Daily Show* producers. Carell offered his own reports, and teaming with Colbert, the two mimicked the shouting matches of 24/7 cable in their debate segment, "Even-Stevphen." The first topic was "Weather: Good or Bad?"

COLBERT: "Every time a Floyd or a Girt lifts their skirt and relieves themselves on the East Coast, Uncle Sam feels obliged to crawl under the plate glass coffee table and throw twenty-dollar bills around. Well, I say 'show's over, folks.' It's time to pull the plug on weather.

CARELL: "Balderdash! The federal government should stay out of the natural disaster business. Today, they're controlling the weather, and tomorrow, who knows? Federal income tax! I'll bet you and your friend Stalin would like that!"

COLBERT: "You, sir, are an idiot, and I'll tell you why: It's time for those fat cats in Washington to get off their keisters and pass legislation outlawing these hurricanes and tornadoes forever. Or maybe, you just hate . . . *children*.

CARELL: "Noooo, I hate you. If tornadoes are outlawed, only outlaws will have tornadoes."

COLBERT: "I'm curious Steve. What's the weather like up your own ass?"

The segment ended with Colbert shouting, "shut up, Shut UP, SHUT UP!" and Carell plugging his ears, chanting "puppy dogs and ice cream!" It soon became a regular feature.

Having brought this little piece of Second City to television, Colbert was planning another transplant. Shortly after Stewart took over, Colbert cut his *Daily Show* appearances to just twenty a year. The extra time allowed him to help Sedaris and Dinello create *The Way After School Special*. In April 1999, "The Three Idiots" debuted the re-titled work, *Strangers with Candy*.

A stranger sitcom has rarely been seen. With footage shot in New Jersey high schools, *Strangers with Candy* featured Jerri Blank, a forty-six-year-old ex-addict who returns to school to get her degree. Sedaris, wearing raccoon eye-makeup and a twisted frown, portrayed Jerri Blank as a warped naïf. Striving to be popular, Jerri sells drugs to classmates, struggles to lose weight, and tries out for homecoming queen. Every episode closed with one of Jerri's moralistic statements, such as:

"I guess what I learned this week was:

- "If you're going to reach for a star, reach for the lowest one you can!"

- "Only losers do drugs, unless it helps you win, and in that case, only winners do drugs!"

- "You never really lose your parents unless, of course, they die, and then they're gone forever, and nothing will bring them back."

Dinello played Geoffrey Jellineck, an insecure art teacher who wants to be as cool as his students. Colbert was Chuck Noblet, a raging, uptight history teacher based on Colbert's former prep school teachers "who wanted to do anything other than teach." And to thicken the melodrama, Noblet and Jellineck were closeted gays. Even Evie Colbert got in on the act, her gentle demeanor adding class to a few cameo roles. *Strangers* got stranger with each episode, drawing cultish fans whom Colbert assumed were "damaged people," but they alienated the critics.

"The show lands with a thud," wrote *The New York Times*. Jerri's blunt lines such as: "I've got to leave early today. I'm having my uterus scraped" were too much for *USA Today*, which found *Strangers* "virtually comedy-free." But the ratings were good enough to get the show renewed for two more seasons. Weirdness, however, has a short shelf life, and *Strangers with Candy* was canceled in October 2000.

With a new century underway, the two sides of Stephen Colbert stood at a crossroads. Looking down one road was the sketch comedian, drawn to performing in skits of Sedaris-style oddity, but he was tiring of snide jokes about small-town eccentrics. Looking down the other road was the faux journalist covering tabloid stories with all the self-importance of CNN. A decade with Dinello and Sedaris had run its course. The "Idiots" were still good friends but had little to show for their collaboration other than cancelations and mixed reviews. They eventually made a forgettable movie version of *Strangers*, but Colbert was finding *The Daily Show* the better road ahead.

Steering the show into the political arena, Stewart encouraged Colbert to make his correspondent persona more topical. Colbert was skeptical. "I thought topical stuff had an ephemeral quality — it would be meaningless in a week." But Stewart "infected me with his spirit of satire," Colbert said, so he began doing more pieces from the studio, often seated beside Stewart. In one, he challenged the charge that the media were feeding kids "a cesspool of sex, vulgarity, and violence." At the word "violence," Colbert reached across the desk to slap Stewart in the face. Parents could not compete with the media in raising children, Colbert said. "We in the entertainment industry have parents *so* outgunned! We've got professional writers, digital networks, global distribution systems! What do you have? A handicam and the love for your child? We will bury you! That's why we must take the children away from their parents and allow them to be raised by the media!"

Colbert could face down parents because he was proving himself a devoted one. Becoming the father he had lost, he doted on his kids - reading to them, playing, and constantly joking. Joy, he said later, is "to be with my wife and children." By the fall of 2000, Stephen, Evie, Madeleine, and Peter Colbert had moved from Westchester County, which they considered too costly, to Montclair, New Jersey. The Colberts appreciated that suburb's fine schools, arts, and proximity to Manhattan.

The move highlighted another contrast between "America's Anchors." While Stewart rode to the *Daily Show*'s midtown office in the backseat of a Comedy Central car, talking on his cell phone to get a head start on each show, Colbert drove to work. He still does. "The network would happily send me home in a car," he told *Vanity Fair*. "After all, they don't want me running off the road. But I'd work the entire way home, and I need more than thirty seconds from the car to the front door to become a dad and a husband again. So I drive home, and I crank my tunes. And by the time I get there, I'm normal again."

As the Colberts settled into their routine – Madeleine in first grade, Peter in pre-school, and a third child, John, born in 2002 – the American media spun out of control. Back when Colbert was working at Second City, weird comedians had little competition. TV news seemed sane, its anchors staid, and the graying men behind the desks considered themselves journalists, not entertainers. In those final, pre-Web years, newspapers were mostly reliable and free of the cluttered competition of Web sites, Tweets, and blogs.

But a decade later, with 24/7 cable spreading and every pol and pundit saying whatever it took to get attention, a comic could scarcely be more outrageous than the media circus. As the age of FOX News and the *Drudge Report* dawned, opinion replaced fact, rumor was treated as truth, and no conspiracy, however trivial or trumped-up, went unnoticed.

Luckily for Colbert, satire has always feasted on fakes and frauds. "I have never made but one prayer to God," Voltaire said. "O Lord, make my enemies ridiculous. And God granted it." Stewart, Colbert, and *The Daily Show* were suddenly blessed with enemies more ridiculous than any god could have provided.

The year 2000 brought another election, but it would not be just another election. Suddenly, after a year of struggling to find a voice, *The Daily Show* team of writers and correspondents spoke as one. Stewart recalled the election as "when I think we tapped into the emotional angle of the news for us and found our editorial footing." In 1996, Craig Kilborn's *Daily Show* had ignored the political conventions, but Stewart insisted on full coverage.

A debut segment - "Indecision 2000" - turned a lackluster campaign into a Swiftian satire of mealymouthed liberals versus uncompassionate conservatives. Senior Political Correspondent Stephen Colbert took it all too seriously. Reporting from the Republican National Convention, Colbert summed up the mood: "Well, Jon, as a journalist I have to maintain my objectivity, but I would say the feeling down here was one of a pervasive and palpable evil: a thick, demonic stench that rolls over you and clings like hot black tar; a nightmare from which you cannot awaken; a nameless fear that lives in the dark spaces beyond your peripheral vision and drives you toward inhuman cruelties and unspeakable perversions. . . ." Then, to emphasize the fakeness of the entire process, Colbert stepped from the convention floor – a space marked by a green screen in the studio - and sat with Stewart at his desk.

But the campaign was just a warm-up for what followed. When the Florida recount spiraled into legal battles over hanging chads, Colbert left his green screen and traveled to the Sunshine State "to cut through the fog of information and facts." There he interviewed voters at a senior citizens' home, calling on "Tiny Turquoise Woman" and "Light Blue Lady." Then, noting that the recount was being compared to a circus sideshow, he found a Florida circus and interviewed the Fat Man, the Fire-Eating Dwarf, and the Snake Charmer.

"Oh, please," the 700-pound Mr. Huge told Colbert, "if anybody ran a sideshow the way Bush and Gore are running this thing, they'd be out of business in a week." Pressed by Colbert, two men whose act consisted of driving spikes into their noses admitted to voting for Bush. "The numbers don't lie," Colbert deadpanned. "While 49 percent of Floridians voted for Gore, 100 percent of Floridians who drive spikes into their heads voted for Bush. Why? Because Bush is the candidate they can relate to."

As the end loomed, Colbert used his nauseated waiter routine to announce the next president, retching and holding back vomit at the name. But the Bush victory provided Colbert with ideal targets for his smarmy sincerity. Suddenly, a swamp full of politicians and pundits were touting themselves as saviors of the nation. Colbert studied them carefully. "I tried to ape whoever was the loudest and the rightest in prime-time cable news," he recalled.

And as Colbert became "the fake newsman's" fake newsman, the journalism establishment noticed. In April 2001, for the first time in history, the George Peabody Award for "distinguished achievement and meritorious service by broadcasters" went to a fake news show, *The Daily Show*, for "Indecision 2000."

Just as Colbert was settling into a steady role, he was stunned by 9/11. Ironically, the date marked the twenty-seventh anniversary of the Colbert family tragedy. Colbert's sister Elizabeth was in Manhattan that morning in a building near the World Trade Center. Fleeing through the debris and chaos, she made it to the Port Authority terminal and took a bus home to Charleston to grieve with her mother. And as if the family had not suffered enough, the aging Lorna Colbert had recently endured another loss, that of her son Billy. The older brother whom Stephen acknowledged as "the joke teller" of the family was a lawyer for the U.S. Treasury Department. Stephen would always remember Billy's love of W.C. Fields and for teaching his youngest brother to juggle. A stroke claimed William "Billy" Colbert at age forty-nine.

Colbert doubts that grief played much of a role in his decision to become a professional funnyman. "There's a common explanation that profound sadness leads to someone's becoming a comedian, but I'm not sure that's a proven equation in my case," he told *The New York Times.* "I'm not bitter about what happened to me as a child, and my mother was instrumental in keeping me from being so. She taught me to be grateful for my life regardless of what that entailed, and that's directly related to the image of Christ on the cross and the example of sacrifice that he gave us."

But the Stephen Colbert who speaks frankly about that 1974 loss of his father and two brothers said nothing about losing a third brother. His faith tested again, he strode into the new century with his persona firmly fixed - the grim nod; the pursed lips; and the rigid, pointed finger. Still, Colbert the sketch comedian found time to pursue more side projects.

During the early Bush years, Colbert was busier than ever. His *Daily Show* work was getting him attention and jobs. He did voice-over work on cartoons and a video game, appeared on *Law and Order* and *Curb Your Enthusiasm*, and hosted two *mockumentaries*, one a rehash of his old stories and the other an *On-Air Guide to Getting on the Air.*

Then, in December 2002, NBC hired Colbert and Stewart to write a sitcom pilot. Set in Colbert's beloved South Carolina, the show was designed to both eulogize and satirize the South, adding gay characters and ethnic jokes to some vague *Mayberry R.F.D.* send-up. NBC thought the script was "too vague" and canceled the project. Then, in 2003, *Daily Show* viewers were startled to see Colbert "searching for Mr. Goodwrench" in commercials for General Motors. Colbert was not proud. "I don't think I can sell out any more than Mr. Goodwrench," he admitted. "I reached an apogee of pimping."

That same year, Colbert teamed with Sedaris and Dinello to write his first book, *Wigfield*, subtitled, *The Can-Do Town That Just May Not. Wigfield* struggled mightily to amuse readers and skewer small towns. The story was told by a purported journalist, Russell Hokes, whose literary tour of Wigfield was a hodgepodge of interviews, oral histories, newspaper articles, and first-person reporting. The message was simple: Small towners are hopeless hicks. That message did not go down well in 2003, as small-town America prepared for war in Iraq. Despite its authors' fame and their nationwide tour in a stage version, *Wigfield* sold poorly.

But Colbert's side projects were mere distractions, given his growing reputation on *The Daily Show*. "Whenever any of his stories ran," former correspondent Bob Wiltfong remembered, "there was a huge reaction from the audience. The feeling among the rest of us was, 'Why is this guy still on the show?'"

Common enemies and a sense of being the sharpest wits on the set cemented the friendship between Colbert and Stewart. They rarely saw each other away from the set, but on camera the two men played off each other like the best comic duos. Colbert accentuated his earnestness with new and distinctive mannerisms - the tilt of the head, the pregnant pause, and the slow, measured pacing towards the camera. Though each report was tightly scripted, a Q-and-A segment following Colbert's opening allowed him to pursue a private goal, that of getting Stewart to break up on camera. "I knew the piece was good if he couldn't look at me when we were at the desk together," Colbert said.

Stewart and Colbert were ideal alter egos. "Jon deconstructs the news," Colbert said. "He's ironic and detached while I falsely construct the news, and I'm ironically attached." Other *Daily Show* correspondents, however, found Stewart and Colbert too attached to each other. "Jon and Stephen were always very friendly and chummy with each other," said Wiltfong. "It always seemed like a world we couldn't get into. . . . Jon just doesn't let many people in, and Stephen was one of the few."

Colbert, however, remained above the jealousy and even the celebrity of his fame. As America careened towards war in Iraq, he was too busy studying the media to worry about private feuds. And when the war came, bringing with it spoon-fed news from embedded reporters, Stewart and Colbert became anchors of ironic protest. "Senior Military Correspondent" Stephen Colbert proved Saddam Hussein was still alive by running a clip of Groucho Marx in the 1933 film, *Duck Soup.* He mocked the futile search for weapons of mass destruction (WMD) by claiming inspectors had found "perfume, Drano, Prell (for moderate to oily hair), and salsa - Tostitos mild, I believe." And when Bush officials finally testified that they had found no WMD in Iraq, Colbert called the announcement "the non-smoking gun we've been looking for."

Come another election year – "Indecision 2004" – Colbert was back in full political mode. His evolution from sketch comic to caricatured correspondent was complete. His reports from the field were funnier, drier, and more distinctive than those of Steve Carell, Samantha Bee, or Ed Helms. Colbert was clearly second-in-command at *The Daily Show,* dwarfed only by his co-anchor. The cacophony of the campaign made humor a daily requirement, thus turning 2004 into "The Year of Jon Stewart." Suddenly, Stewart was everywhere - on magazine covers, *60 Minutes,* even *Crossfire,* where his blistering attack became an Internet sensation. Colbert stayed in Stewart's shadow, filing report after report - his future waiting in the wings.

With America mired in a controversial war, cable news became a verbal mosh pit. Bill O'Reilly, Sean Hannity, Rush Limbaugh, Laura Ingraham, and others were openly insulting guests and spewing false facts, causing the ghost of Edward R. Murrow to spin in his grave. Who would take these high priests and priestesses of punditry down a notch?

Periodically throughout 2004, *The Daily Show* previewed a new program, *The Colbert Report.* The clips showed a strident Colbert shouting, sneering, and not just adjusting his glasses, but ripping them from his face. In his nastiest voice, Colbert announced, "Tonight, I sit down with top newsmakers and tell them to SHUT THE HELL UP!" Colbert denounced guests as being an "Idiot!" or a "Jackass!" and he played off O'Reilly's "No Spin Zone" by suggesting a "No-Fact Zone." In a supposed interview with the Dalai Lama, Colbert asked, "What the heck do you know about world peace, baldy? SHUT UPPPPP!" More *Colbert Report* segments aired, but Stewart called them "previews of an exciting new *Daily Show* spin-off that's already been canceled."

America, however, needed *The Colbert Report.* The election had hardened the divide between the so-called red states and blue states, and the partisan bickering was left to caricature itself. "Shut up" became not just a Colbert joke, but an attention-getter. Right-wing pundits became best-selling authors and full-blown celebrities. If only Colbert could break out of parody. If only he could embody the strength and virility of Stone Phillips, the sense of mission of Geraldo Rivera, and the crusading warrior spirit of Bill O'Reilly. Such a caricature would be more than the high-status idiot Colbert had played since his time with Second City. This evolving egomaniac would mock all that Stewart and Colbert saw as being wrong with America and its flaming media. Pompous, full of himself, oblivious to facts, the emerging Colbert would be a hybrid of many different media personalities. Such a character just might find an audience.

CHAPTER 5
TRUTHINESS

*"I used to make up stuff in my bio all the time –
that I used to be a professional ice-skater and stuff
like that. I found it so inspirational. Why not
make myself cooler than I am?"*

Mention George Orwell and the title of his dystopian novel on totalitarianism will soon follow. Fears of "Big Brother" are still invoked whenever government surveillance is mentioned, yet *1984* remains a work of fiction. It is another Orwell work, "Politics and the English Language," that describes our current state of affairs.

In that essay, Orwell argued that "the English language is in a bad way." Language matters, he said, because it links rhetoric to reality. When rhetoric is detached from reality, the consequences extend far beyond the classroom and the reading room. "Now, it is clear that the decline of a language must ultimately have political and economic causes," Orwell wrote. ". . . [B]ut an effect can become a cause, reinforcing the original cause and producing the same effect in an intensified form, and so on indefinitely. A man may take to drink because he feels himself to be a failure, and then fail all the more completely because he drinks. It is rather the same thing that is happening to the English language. It becomes ugly and inaccurate because our thoughts are foolish, but the slovenliness of our language makes it easier for us to have foolish thoughts."

By 2005, America's media landscape resembled Orwell's drunk. Ugly language was daily fare. Foolish thoughts were passed off as gospel, and each person had his own set of facts. Best-selling memoirs were found to contain invented scenes, and major publications, including *The Atlantic* and *The New York Times,* admitted to publishing fabricated stories. A new online encyclopedia, Wikipedia, allowed anyone to amend any article with little fact-checking. A billion blogs filled the Internet, each blogger holding fast to some hometown version of truth.

Nearly half of all Americans did not believe in evolution, and an equally shocking number thought global warming was a hoax. No one seemed to trust anyone, except the one source each trusted, whom no one else trusted. Was all truth relative?

Were scientific theories, even those endorsed by the scientific community, just maybes? Were facts, as Ronald Reagan once misstated, just "stupid things?"

When *The Colbert Report* was first conceived, *Daily Show* producers considered it a passing skit. But shortly after the 2004 election, Colbert began to worry. "I thought, 'Well, I've been through two election cycles here; I've been here a long time. I still love it but I'm not sure how much longer I'll love it.'" He still wanted to work with Stewart, but how?

Capitalizing on his skyrocketing celebrity, Stewart had contracted with Comedy Central to create a new show. So together with his head writer, Ben Karlin, Stewart began to see *The Colbert Report* as something more than a skit.

Cable TV's prevailing pundit, Bill O'Reilly, had just been accused of sexual harassment. Having settled out of court for an undisclosed sum, O'Reilly was unrepentant and the case was hopelessly muddled. Who knew whom to believe? Who would ever know? And was there no limit to celebrity ego?

In January 2005, as the nation braced for a second Bush term, Stewart and Karlin approached Doug Herzog, president of Comedy Central, to propose a spin-off of *The Daily Show*. The pitch was brief. It took Herzog just a few minutes to see the possibilities. Stewart, Carlin, and Colbert spent the next few months hammering out the details of *The*

Colbert Report. The dozen clips already aired on *The Daily Show* were a start, but they seemed too strident. A sniping pundit telling everyone to "shut up!" might be funny for a moment, but he couldn't carry a half-hour show.

Colbert's character would have to be broader, deeper, more farcical. He would have to take himself *sooo* seriously that no one else could take him seriously. Shamelessly waving the flag, drenching his stage in eagles, bunting, and other symbols of freedom, he would be a living symbol of the simple-minded people who claim exclusive rights to the words "truth," "patriot," and "American." He would be angry, but not for long; critical, but only in jest. He would be, as Colbert said, "well intentioned but poorly informed." And above all, while mastering the current political jargon, he would have to call attention to its distortions. Was a former sketch comedian up to such a role?

The Colbert Report was announced in May 2005. It would, said Comedy Central president Herzog, be "our version of the *O'Reilly Factor* with Stephen Colbert." For those unfamiliar with the name, it was explained as Colbear, with a soft 't'. And Repore, with a parallel ending. The *Daily Show* promos featured Colbert sneering, "It's French, bitch," but that idea was cut. Too mean. *The Colbert Report* would debut in October, the press was told, for an eight-week trial run.

Colbert went to work finding role models. He was already in awe of O'Reilly, who he called "Papa Bear." "I'd love to be able to put a chain of words together the way he does," Colbert said, "without much thought as to what it might mean, compared to what you said about the same subject the night before." But no show could survive with only one model, so Colbert also watched Hannity, Ann Coulter, Michael Savage - a whole murder of crowing cable pundits. And while he watched, the American rhetoric grew still more strident, more Orwellian.

"Conservative asshole!"

"Liberal fuckhead!"

"Fuck you!"

"No, fuck you!"

"Would everyone please just shut up, SHUT UP, SHUUUUTTTTTT UPPPPPPPPPPPPPPP!"

On October 17, 2005, a day on which nothing of even the slightest importance occurred, Stewart closed *The Daily Show* with a promo for an upcoming program "with our own Stephen Colbert." The camera cut to Colbert at his desk.

"Stephen, we're really excited about the show tonight," Stewart said.

"Me, too, Jon. I really feel like I'm going to make a lot of money doing this."

Moments later, viewers who stayed tuned saw a different Colbert, one who seemed injected with testosterone. Gone was the stern, earnest correspondent. Buried deep was the sketch comedian. Stepping – no, leaping - to the front was the president of Colbert Nation. Commanding the camera by approaching it from askew, Colbert revealed his top stories. The last headline said it all: "Finally, a new television show premieres and changes - the - world! Open wide, Baby Bird, 'cause Mama's got a big fat night crawler of truth. Here comes the *Colbert Report.*"

The now familiar opening showed the once shy, nerdy fantasy fan giving the American flag a full-body, Iwo Jima wave, all but bitch-slapping the camera. Then the camera cut to Colbert at his desk. Sure, his name was on the set, he began, and it was overhead, on the screen in front of him, on chaser lights, on either side of the desk, it shaped like a giant "C." But this was not about him. *The Colbert Report* was dedicated to the heroes. "And who are the heroes?" he asked. "The people who watch this show," Colbert declared - average hard-working Americans. You're not the elite. You're not the country-club crowd. I know for a fact that my country club would never let you in. But you *get it.* And you come from a long line of it-getters. You

come from a line of folks who say somethings –
got – to – be – done. Well, you're doing something
right now. You're - watching - television. And on
this show, your voice will be heard - in - the form
of my voice."

It was a modest beginning, but what followed would
forever be Colbert's trademark. With little fanfare,
he introduced Tonight's Word: "Truthiness." "Now
I'm sure some of the word police, the 'Wordinistas'
over at Webster's, will say, 'Hey, that's not a word.'
Well, anybody who knows me knows that I'm no
fan of dictionaries *or* reference books. They're
elitist, constantly telling us what is or isn't true, or
what did or didn't happen." Colbert moved on to
the routine he would soon perform just a dozen
paces from the President of the United States:
"More nerve endings in your gut than your brain.
Look it up in your gut." He gave examples of Bush
decisions that, if you *thought* about them, were
absurd, but if you *felt* them, they seemed like right
moves. "The truthiness is, anyone can read the
news *to* you. I promise to *feel* the news *at* you." And
a lexicon was born.

Others had tried to sum up the slippery nature of
truth in the cable age. "Factoids." "Tabloid truths."
"Bullshit," as in the 2005 bestseller, *On Bullshit*. But
Colbert had come up with a term - *the* term - that
would endure. And he had coined it just two hours
before taping his first show.

During the 4:00 p.m. rehearsal, the "Word of the Day" had been "truth," which Colbert planned to contrast with those annoying "facts." But he decided "truth" was not "dumb" enough. "I wanted a silly word that would feel wrong in your mouth," he said. Thinking for a minute, he had it: truthiness. And like the lie that, as Mark Twain said, "gets halfway around the world before truth puts on its boots," truthiness began its march through American culture.

Most newspapers praised Colbert's debut. "A hilarious send-up of TV news' puffed-up pundit class," said the *Philadelphia Inquirer.* "Occasionally brilliant, occasionally loopy, definitely entertaining," said the *Houston Chronicle.* A few did not get the joke. "It feels like a weaker extension of *The Daily Show*," judged the *Seattle Post-Intelligencer.* But truthiness was here to stay. Rarely has a recent coinage been so quickly and universally embraced. Journalists began using truthiness whenever truth proved less than, well, truthy. The word surfaced on ABC's *Nightline, USA Today, The Washington Post, Newsweek,* CNN, MSNBC, *Fox News,* the Associated Press, *Editor & Publisher, Salon,* and *The Huffington Post.* "We live in the age of truthiness," *New York Times* columnist Frank Rich observed. And in January 2006, the American Dialect Society agreed, naming truthiness its Word of the Year. Runners-up included "Katrina," "podcast," "intelligent design," and "disaster industrial complex."

Lexicographers noted that truthiness was not a new word. Unbeknownst to Colbert, it had been used sparingly since 1824. But the word fit the times and became immortal. By 2010, it could be found in several dictionaries, but the Wordinistas at Webster's still left it out of their dictionaries. The authoritative Oxford English Dictionary, however, defined truthiness as "the quality of seeming or being felt to be true, even if not necessarily true." The OED noted the word's use in the nineteenth century but gave "U.S. humorist Stephen Colbert" credit for its popularization in "the modern sense."

Comedy Central had expected to wait out the eight-week trial run to consider the fate of *The Colbert Report*, but truthiness, combined with Colbert's sassiness, made the show an instant hit. *The Daily Show* had taken six years and "The Year of Jon Stewart" in 2004 to amass its nightly audience of 2.5 million. But from the first week of the *Report*, some 80 percent of *Daily Show* viewers stayed tuned to Colbert. Just two weeks after the debut, Comedy Central renewed the show for a year.

"I want to *thank* Comedy Central for picking up the show," Colbert said. "This says really good things about you guys. You clearly 'get it.'" Some thought Colbert's caricature could not carry a half-hour show. Colbert himself worried about seeming too critical or partisan. "I don't think he's necessarily a Republican or Democrat," he said of his character. "He is part of the 'Blame America Last' crowd." Colbert had known strident conservatives in Charleston, at Hampden-Sydney, even at Northwestern, and he knew they weren't much fun to be around. As the lone presence before the camera, Colbert knew that however loony he might seem, he would have to be likable. "If you try to maintain your humanity when you do the jokes, and not play on tragedy or cynically dismiss people's beliefs, then I think people will, hopefully, respect your attempt to stay civil."

But could such a simplistic figure outlast TV's incessant demand for the new? Producer Ben Karlin saw vast potential. "We've got some stuff coming up that will really continue to expand the universe more and more and more, and make people realize that this is not just a parody," Karlin said.

Throughout the rest of 2005 and into 2006, American rhetoric got uglier and uglier. The contrast between what was said and who was saying it suggested Oscar Wilde's novel *The Picture of Dorian Gray*. Like the eponymous Dorian, the faces that delivered the news remained handsome, beautiful, and beaming. But as they descended into more mudslinging, their portrait of America became deformed and demonic. Liberals were "godless" and "stinking scum." Conservatives were "right-wing lunatics" and "conservative fuckwads." Now, however, there was an alternative to shut up,

Shut UP, SHUUUUTTTTTT UPPPPPPPPP! There was Stephen Colbert.

Colbert spent the first months on the air doing what any good political figure must, solidifying his base. Because his base was initially built on *The Daily Show*, Stewart ran nightly promos for Colbert's upcoming show. But as *The Colbert Report* expanded its universe, it slowly diverged from Stewart. Stewart mocked the right-wing media, but Colbert *became* the right-wing media. He answered its relentless fear-mongering with periodic "Threat Downs" listing the five biggest threats to America and "reminding you to cower in fear." He answered caustic critics with the series, "Who's Attacking Me Now?" And he soothed fears of falling behind the news cycle with a regular segment, "All You Need to Know." "Yesterday, the Kansas Board of Education approved new science standards for public schools that would allow teachers to offer lessons on intelligent design. All you need to know in Kansas? Evidently very little."

Yet Colbert was still an anchorman at a desk until he did an interview. Stewart's political clout was earning him interviews with diplomats, Nobel Prize winners, even foreign heads of state. Stewart slipped a few jokes into each interview but treated eminent guests with respect. Colbert would have none of that. He saw the interview as a chance to use his Second City skills.

"The trouble with the jokes," Colbert said, "is that once they're written, I know how they're supposed to work, and all I can do is not hit them. I'm more comfortable improvising. If I have just two or three ideas and I know how the character feels, what the character wants, everything in between is like trapeze work." Colbert's improv interviews became a new art form, pitting him against guests unaware they had been invited to improvise. His "Better Know a District" segment sprung his trap on one unwitting politician after another. Florida Congressman Robert Wexler's hapless defense of the caribou Colbert wanted to "grind up and put in my tank" was just the beginning.

To interview congressmen in their natural habitat, Colbert began flying to Washington, D.C., conducting a few "Better Know a District" interviews with each visit. He warned congressmen, as he still does with all guests, that "my character is an idiot." Politicians, however, did not see him coming. Skillful editing, audience laughter, and Colbert's quickness made congressman after congressman look foolish. Nebraska's Representative Lee Terry never understood Colbert's double *entendres* about Omaha's meatpacking industry.

> "What's going on with American beef and the Japanese markets right now?"

> "Not much. Japan has banned our beef."

"What are you trying to do to get Japan to receive your meat?"

"It is a diplomatic issue of trying to get them to simply let us sell beef again."

"How is the meat delivered?"

"Well, it depends on what you want. You can have a small cut or a larger cut. You can keep it hard with the bone in it."

"Is it delivered hot?"

"You can get it as hot as you want."

Some congressmen smiled, others seethed. Massachusetts's Barney Frank, known in Congress for his caustic wit, scowled as Colbert danced around his sexuality. Frank is openly gay, but Colbert pretended not to know. He asked Frank about the awkwardness of being liberal, Jewish, and left-handed. Then Colbert added, "There's something else about you - and this is sort of the elephant in the room I'm not naming . . . you're a little overweight." Later, when Frank mentioned his "boyfriend," Colbert was shocked. "Oh, you're a homosexual." He apologized, then apologized for apologizing. Finally Colbert said, "It seems like fewer and fewer people are upset, or frightened by homosexuals. What can homosexuals do to re-instill people with an irrational fear?"

Frank found the question silly and ended the

interview. "I like political humor," Frank said later, "but I found this really strange. His basic interview technique was to pretend he didn't know things. That wouldn't be funny in junior high school."

District by district, Colbert laid siege to Congress. House Speaker Nancy Pelosi warned fellow congressmen: "Don't subject yourself to a comic's edit unless you want to be made a fool of." But Nebraska's Lee Terry saw his appearance with Colbert as "a way for my constituents to see me in something other than an opponent's 30-second attack ad." And the audience's response? "I've never had as many people, i.e., potential voters, approach me on the street as I have had since my appearance on *The Colbert Report*. As for subjecting myself to a comic's edit, I would much rather have my words taken out of context by Stephen Colbert than by the 'real' media. At least with Mr. Colbert, the context is clearly comedy, and the audience gets it."

Colbert Nation agreed, and "Better Know a District" is still making its way through the 435 congressional districts. It remains a popular *Colbert Report* feature.

Colbert was kinder to studio guests. Those interviews, done without editing, worried him. "I thought that the interviews would be the thing I hated the most." He knew he would have to be tough on politicos, quick with celebrities, and softer on authors and academics. Could he "dial it up" and "dial it down?" "I'm not an assassin," he said. "Even though my character's very aggressive and I have a satirical intent, I don't want them to feel unwelcome." But he found the challenge invigorating, and nightly interviews soon became Colbert's favorite part of each "*Report*."

Once Colbert finished his victory lap around the studio, as if the audience was applauding for him, his interviews managed to be both funny and respectful. And with his ratings rising, his show became a vital stop for anyone promoting a book, movie, or policy. They came from all political persuasions - from Al Sharpton and Ralph Nader on the left to Peggy Noonan and Bill Kristol on the right. Regardless of political persuasion, each guest noticed what Colbert himself soon touted, the "Colbert Bump." After appearing on Colbert, authors sold more books, musicians' CD sales spiked, and politicians raked in campaign contributions. No Colbert Bump, however, rivaled the one he gave himself as keynote speaker at the White House Correspondents' Dinner.

The annual dinner for presidents and reporters dates to 1920. Down through the decades, guests have included Frank Sinatra, Bob Hope, James Cagney, and Barbra Streisand. Yet only with the presidency of Ronald Reagan, veteran of Hollywood roasts, did the correspondents' dinner itself become a good-natured roasting. Rich Little, Jay Leno, Conan O'Brien, and even Jon Stewart, before *The*

Daily Show, had stepped to the podium to make lighthearted fun of the president. The atmosphere was formal - black tie - but the rules were unwritten. A comedian could mock a president's personality but not his policies. Sarcasm was okay, satire was not. Either no one explained these rules to Colbert, or he ignored them. And because his conservative caricature was less known than his *Daily Show* correspondent, it's possible the Correspondents Association thought the earlier Colbert would show up. When it was all over, when President George W. Bush was done seething and Colbert was hailed as "one of the great satirical wits of our time," the journalist who invited Colbert admitted he hadn't seen much of *The Colbert Report.*

Many Colbert fans admit he was not at his best that night. Some jokes fell with a thud; others glanced off the audience. The silence between jokes was awkward. But tens of millions of Americans had waited a very long time for that moment. By April 2006, George W. Bush had been president for five years, and to a growing number of disgusted citizens, those five years had seemed like an eternity. In the wake of 9/11, with its shock and sorrow, Bush had led a relentless and reckless march to war. Then came the "shock and awe" of the Iraq invasion, the arrogance of power – "Democracy is messy!" - and Bush's macho "Mission Accomplished" speech amidst a bumbling aftermath. Oops, there were no weapons of mass destruction. "Those weapons of mass destruction have got to be somewhere," Bush actually joked. "Nope, no weapons over there . . . maybe under here?" Oh, and that yellow-cake uranium Saddam bought in Africa? Never mind. Abu Ghraib and the tortured prisoners? "Just a few bad apples." Further denials were followed by Katrina and assorted gaffes, foreign and domestic.

Just weeks before the dinner, Bush had claimed, "I'm the decider, and I decide what's best." Would no one stand up and give this man the mocking he deserved?

Before the dinner, the entire Colbert family, including Lorna Colbert, met Bush at a private party. "We actually had a very nice conversation beforehand about the nature of irony," Colbert remembered. "The president was charming and lovely. The president's mother went to the same school as my wife. He was extremely nice to my mom. I have beautiful pictures of the two of them together that night. Nice guy."

But once Colbert stepped to the podium, it was "no more Mr. Nice Guy." His mock praise dug deep. Colbert lauded "my president" for being consistent. "He believes the same thing Wednesday that he believed on Monday, no matter what happened Tuesday." Colbert pretended to be appalled at criticism of White House personnel changes. Bush was not "re-arranging deck chairs on the Titanic. This administration is not sinking,"

Colbert pleaded. "This administration is soaring. If anything, they are rearranging the deck chairs on the Hindenburg."

While most cameras fixed on Colbert, one stayed riveted on Bush. It showed him leaning back in his chair, lips pursed, occasionally chuckling but mostly looking as if he had that proverbial poker up his ass. A White House aide saw the president "ready to blow." But Bush remained calm, dignified, presidential. When the roast was finished, Bush stood along with the rest of the head table and shook Colbert's hand. "Well done," he said as the comedian passed.

Sitting down, however, Colbert sensed something wrong. No one in the audience would look at him. Some were embarrassed; others were shocked. Only a few were bemused. "Colbert," one White House aide said, "crossed the line."

When the dinner ended, Colbert had no idea what he had unleashed. Exhausted, he went back to his hotel, slept, and headed home to Montclair. The following Monday morning, he met with his writers to plan another show. Noticing that he seemed blasé about the dinner, one said, "Have you looked at the Internet?" Writers began sending him links to the Web sites that were taking *Colbert v. Bush* viral. He read a few but found them mixed and asked not to be sent any more. The mainstream press had little on his speech, and what little they had was mixed. "Colbert was not just a failure as a comedian, but rude," said the *Washington Post*. Most newspapers ignored the speech, however, leading some in Colbert Nation to denounce a "media blackout" as payback for Colbert's criticism of reporters. No such blackout existed. Reporters on deadline simply found it easier to characterize the evening by describing Bush's own performance alongside a Bush impersonator.

Only when the Internet lit up did the press follow. Reporters watched the footage online. A few sloughed off their lack of coverage, saying Colbert had bombed, but all admired his courage. Beneath the headline, "Stephen Colbert Has Brass *Cojones*," the *San Francisco Chronicle* wrote: "Stephen Colbert of *The Colbert Report* just made himself about 500 times more of a national treasure and cemented himself as one of the most fearless satirists of this generation (instantly outpacing Jon Stewart, who, you get the feeling, wouldn't have had the nerve to go as far as Colbert did) by way of a savage and hilarious roast/takedown of President Bush who was seated not eight feet away. Have you heard? Did you see? You simply must. It was a revelation."

As revelation, as iTunes bestseller, as gatherer of millions of YouTube hits, Colbert's performance had nailed the president and his endless war. Six months later, *New York Times* columnist Frank Rich called it a "defining moment" of "the '*Colbert*' election, so suffused is it with unreality, or what Mr. Colbert calls 'truthiness.'"

Colbert took the White House dinner in stride. On the next *Colbert Report*, he aired clips of his Hindenburg joke and shots of the audience straight-faced. "The crowd practically carried me out on their shoulders," he joked, "although I wasn't actually ready to leave." But the bump Colbert had given himself sent him soaring beyond truthiness. By 2007, his audience was growing as quickly as his reputation. Here was a comedian who transcended mere comedy, a satirist with the *cojones* to take on anyone, and a media genius whose innovative use of TV skewered America's celebrity-sated culture. After one decade on small stages and another in the shadow of Jon Stewart, Stephen Colbert "got it."

CHAPTER 6
"THE JOY MACHINE"

"Hey, America, are you thinking what I'm thinking? You soon will be."

Colbert Nation was both larger and smaller than it seemed. Larger because the nation Stephen Colbert addressed four nights a week had more viewers than ever. Smaller because Colbert Nation was geographically compact. Colbert could cross it in twenty minutes, and he did so each morning and evening.

Stephen and Evie still live in upper-middle-class Montclair, New Jersey, where they moved in 2000. Their children attend Montclair public schools. Madeleine is college age; *Peter* is starting high school, and *John* will soon head to middle school.

None looks much like their father. The boys both have Evie's brown hair and large eyes. Colbert did not let his children watch either *The Daily Show* or *The Colbert Report*. "I truck in insincerity," he told *60 Minutes*. "With a very straight face, I say things I don't believe. Kids can't understand irony or sarcasm, and I don't want them to perceive me as insincere."

The same contrast between Colbert on- and off-camera frequently catches Montclair residents off guard. Few recognize him as the blathering idiot he played on *The Colbert Report*. Blending into his town, Colbert teaches Sunday school, works out in a gym, and attends local plays and charity benefits. Everyone who meets him is surprised to shake hands with a soft-spoken gentleman. "I think they always want to meet the guy who's going to show up and tell jokes," Colbert said. "But if I'm asked to do something that isn't specifically a performance, then I have to be very specific that he's never going to show up."

Stephen Colbert, the prattling fool, did not live in Montclair, New Jersey. He lived only in Colbert Nation. So each morning, when Stephen Colbert - good father, good citizen, and good Catholic – dropped his kids off at school, headed for the gym, and then headed to work, he had to consult his character en route. The drive from Montclair into Manhattan took the two Colberts through the Midtown Tunnel, then north a dozen blocks to West 54th Street in Hell's Kitchen. There, in a three-story brick office building, just around the corner from The *Daily Show* headquarters, the Stephen Colbert who greeted his staff was the serious and sober one, not the joker, not until the camera went on.

With a cast of one and a crew of eighty, *The Colbert Report* was an efficient machine. Colbert liked to call it "the joy machine," and its parts were already in motion by the time he arrived at 11:00 a.m. His writers, an intelligent and intensely ironic crew, mostly in their late twenties and early thirties, had spent the morning eating cold cereal, perusing headlines, and scanning TiVo clips. Writers met formally at 9:30 a.m. to pick the day's top stories.

When Colbert arrived, the place shifted into high gear. In his *Lord of the Rings*-studded office, which also included a lightsaber given to him by George Lucas and a signed photo of Democrat George McGovern, Colbert met with his head writers to discuss the evening's show. Once the day's headlines and horrors had been channeled into ongoing segments: "Tip of the Hat, Wag of the Finger," "Cheating Death," "Better Know a . . ." or any of a dozen more segments, the writers went to work. Scripts were due at 1:00 p.m., at which point some jokes would be revised, others jettisoned or saved for another day. Any late-breaking news would be added.

All *Report* employees agreed that the twelve-hour days and deadline pressure made for a grueling "joy machine," but they also agreed that Colbert was an ideal boss. Keeping his character in the wings, Colbert remained congenial throughout the afternoon, lending his timing and intellect to each developing skit. Everyone on the set, aka "the eagle's nest," was astounded by his knowledge. Fueled by his childhood book-a-day habit, Colbert remains a devout reader who retains prodigious quantities of raw information about Catholic saints, song lyrics, American history, Tolkien trivia, and more. But co-workers were equally astounded by how down-to-earth this superstar remained.

"There are a lot of unhappy people in comedy," says Tom Purcell, *The Colbert Report* executive producer, "and sometimes you get a very radioactive vibe. But Stephen has an excellent way of treating people." Writer Peter Grosz adds that Colbert is "amazingly easy to write for because he has an incredibly open mind. He wants to hear all ideas and has lots of faith and trust in his writers, and he expects that anything coming out of your mouth is going to be something worth listening to."

By 5:15 p.m., when the show was ready for rehearsal, Colbert prepared himself to become HIMSELF. "You can't be 'Stephen Colbert' all day because he'd be a terrible executive producer," he says. "Right before they call me for the show, I have a special button that I push on my side that releases the gas."

Alone in his dressing room, Colbert checked his tie in the mirror. If the show's guest had arrived in the Green Room, he would visit to warn that his character was "an idiot" and to just play along. Then he headed out to meet the studio audience. Already warmed up by a producer, the crowd exploded when Colbert appeared. He talked for a few minutes, not in character, then sat inside his trademark C-desk for a run through. By 7:00 p.m., the show was ready for taping. Cameras lurched into action, and Colbert pivoted to catch each at a different angle. Blaring credits rolled to the dissonant notes of "Baby Mumbles" by Cheap Trick. All attention was on Colbert. It often took a full minute for the crowd to stop chanting "Steee-Phen! Steee-Phen! Steee-Phen!"

For the next two hours, with takes and re-takes, Colbert Nation was neither a metaphor nor a concept. It is as real as each laugh, as united as each ovation. When the taping was finished, Colbert headed home, listening to music as he drove back through the Lincoln Tunnel, back to Montclair, back to his home where Evie and the kids were waiting.

Though time is said to "wait for no man," it sometimes seemed to stand still on *The Colbert Report*. Each half-hour passed quickly, but the show itself seemed ageless. When first asked to do headline humor on *The Daily Show*, Colbert resisted, wanting his character to be "eternal." But "eternal" seemed to be the goal of his own show. Headlines changed, spoofs came and went, but a *Colbert Report* from 2006 looked remarkably like a *Report* when the show ended in December 2014. The set had not changed, nor had the format or the host.

Jon Stewart was aging gracefully, his hair graying a little each year, but even though Colbert's hair began to gray shortly after he took on the show, it was in 2014 as dark as it was on *Exit 57*. As he approached fifty, Colbert was slightly leaner and his face more seasoned. Yet he still exuded energy on camera, racing around the set, bursting with joy, coyly eyeing the camera as if still a boy competing in his family's "humorocracy." Some saw stagnation in the day-to-day sameness of *The Colbert Report,* but within the familiar framework, Colbert remained a master of improv.

In the years since his Bush-bashing made him a phenomenon, Colbert had broken down television's so-called fourth wall between performer and audience. Colbert might well have rested on his laurels. A partial list of his awards include two Emmys, two Peabodys, Associated Press Celebrity of the Year (2007), two *New York Times'* bestselling books, a Grammy, numerous honorary degrees, and, for some reason, a spot on *Maxim's* 100 Sexiest Women (number sixty-nine).

Instead of stagnating, however, Colbert kept viewers guessing about what he might do next. The sheer fun he had on camera is part of *The Colbert Report*'s appeal. As if living by Second City's improv strategy – "Yes, and . . ." – Colbert was open to all suggestions. And as if following his family motto, "Never refuse a legitimate adventure," he continued to delight viewers with one adventure after another. He rode a bobsled with the U.S. Olympic team, sang with Willie Nelson and Paul McCartney, and let Jane Fonda climb in his lap and nibble his ear. He challenged actor Sean Penn to a "meta-free-phor-all," issued "green screen challenges," invited viewers to use his image in their own videos, and taught Bill Clinton how to Tweet.

Colbert's biggest gamble, however, came in 2009, when he took the *Report* to Iraq to perform for American troops. Colbert allowed the Army to put him through a very basic, Basic Training, but even that was not sufficiently adventurous. "If you really want to be in the military," General Ray Odierno told him before a crowd of soldiers, "you're going to have to get your haircut like these guys out here."

"I don't know about that, sir."

"Stephen, if you want to do this right, you're gonna have to get your hair cut."

"But without my hair, what would I blow dry? And frankly, sir, it's gonna take more than a four-star general to get me to cut my hair."

Static emerged offstage, followed by President Obama on a big screen. "If Stephen Colbert wants to play soldier," Obama declared, "it's time to cut that man's hair."

"Sir, is that an order?" General Odierno asked.

"General, as your commander-in-chief, I hereby order you to shave that man's head."

Game for anything that would get a laugh, Colbert sat still while the general's buzzing clippers mowed off his hair. For the next several weeks, the crew cut served as a reminder of the Iraq adventure and made Stephen Colbert seem still more human.

Each *Report* may have looked the same, but many contained transformative moments when "Colbert the caricature" became "Colbert the marketing genius." Blending TV with the Internet, social media, and his own vivid imagination, Colbert continually challenged his "nation" to take action. Some actions scaled the heights of the human ego.

A few months after *Colbert v. Bush* went viral, Colbert learned of an online contest to name a bridge across the Danube River in Hungary. Early voting had "The Chuck Norris Bridge" in the lead, but then Colbert told his fans to vote to name the bridge after him. A week later, with only 1,774 votes, Colbert gave more explicit voting instructions. Overnight, Colbert Nation poured online and moved him into second place with 438,039 votes.

He then added a link to his own Web site that bypassed the hurdle of the Hungarian language.

"I think if we hit 100 million votes, I get to be prime minister," he told his nation. A week later, the "Stephen Colbert Bridge" had some 17 million votes. Colbert then called off the campaign, noting that 17 million "is 7 million more than there are in the country of Hungary." The Hungarian government, however, refused to go along with the gag, changing the rules to allow only names of dead Hungarians. Colbert pretended to be outraged, but later hosted the Hungarian ambassador on the *Report*. "He made me an honorary citizen and invited me to speak at their parliament," Colbert said. "That's when I realized we had something special with our audience."

In subsequent years, Colbert Nation had gone online to append Colbert's name to a Michigan hockey team, and the "Combined Operational Load-Bearing External Resistance Treadmill (COLBERT)" on the International Space Station. The treadmill was a compromise offered by NASA after Colbert handily won its online contest to name a room on the space station. Colbert had also lobbied for himself, talking guests into appending his name to an airliner, a spider, an eagle, a beetle, and a gift shop in Alabama. His unbridled ego was contagious. Almost everyone wanted in on a Colbert joke. Everyone except Wikipedia, that is.

Founded in 2001, Wikipedia was still struggling for acceptance in July 2006 when Colbert took out a laptop and showed viewers how easy it was to alter the site's content. The online encyclopedia, whose wiki technology allows anyone to edit any entry, seemed the perfect target for truthiness. "I love Wikipedia," Colbert announced. "Any site that's got a longer entry on 'truthiness' than on Lutherans has its priorities straight."

He then introduced the "Word of the Day," "Wikiality." Slapping his laptop's keyboard, Colbert pretended to change Wikipedia's entry on George Washington to read that the first president had not owned slaves. If enough people agree on "Wikiality," he said, it becomes reality. "What we're doing is bringing democracy to knowledge." He then told his nation to log onto Wikipedia, search "elephant," and add that the number of elephants in Africa had tripled in the past six months. "It's the least we can do to save this noble beast. Together, we can create a reality we can agree on - the reality we just agreed on."

Colbert's wiki campaign broke down another wall, the wall between television and the Internet. Most TV shows had Web sites, but Colbert was the first to send viewers to sites other than his own. When Colbert Nation crashed Wikipedia's servers, Wikipedia responded by locking its entries on "elephants," blocking access to entries about

Colbert and his show, and banning the user name "stephencolbert." Colbert backed off, only to return a few months later to announce that someone had broken through: Wikipedia's entry on elephants read, "Thanks to the works of Stephen Colbert, the population has tripled in the last ten years."

Colbert later urged viewers to amend Wikipedia's "Warren Harding" entry by adding that Harding had been a "secret Negro president." In 2011, Colbert Nation amended Wikipedia's "Paul Revere" entry, adding "pealing bells" to his midnight ride, as Sarah Palin had recently claimed.

Behind Colbert the prankster, his eye twinkling at each new gambit, stood Colbert the *p*hilanthropist. True to what he told Stewart moments before his first *Report*, Colbert had made "a lot of money doing this." His earnings started with his annual $4.5 million Comedy Central salary, plus residuals from various voice-overs in films. He also earned plenty from his best-selling books, *I Am America (and So Can You)* and *America Again: Re-becoming the Greatness We Never Weren't.* Then there were the *Tek Jansen* comic book series based on Colbert as a superhero. Add up the earnings and the man who once used his infant daughter as an audition prop now raked in $6 million a year. The figure put Colbert's earnings far below those of top celebrities, yet few had been more generous with their time, and none had been as creative in raising money for charity.

On October 18, 2006, the first anniversary of the *Report*, Colbert auctioned the portrait of himself that hung over the fireplace on his set. A Charleston, South Carolina, barbecue restaurant paid a cool $50,605 and hung the portrait in its lobby. At Colbert's request, all proceeds went to *the* Save the Children charitable organization. A year later, when Colbert fell on the set and broke his wrist, he had guests sign the cast, then sold it on eBay, with proceeds going to the Yellow Ribbon Fund that helps American soldiers returning from active duty abroad.

Colbert soon found a charity that remains his favorite, Donors Choose, which lets anyone donate directly to specific projects for needy public schools. Colbert first used the DonorsChoose.org site during the 2008 Pennsylvania Democratic primary. He asked his viewers to cast their votes online for candidates Barack Obama or Hillary Clinton; then he referred them to Donors Choose. What he called his "Celebrate the Democalypse" campaign raised $185,000 for Pennsylvania public schools. Colbert continued to raise six-figure sums for Donors Choose, sending huge quantities of supplies to children who sent him their drawings in return. In 2009, he joined the charity's board of directors.

In 2012, Colbert gave royalties from his children's book, *I Am a Pole (And So Can You!)*, to U.S. Vets, a group that provides basic services to veterans. Proceeds from the sales of his Ben & Jerry's ice cream flavor, Stephen Colbert's Americone Dream, are also distributed to charity. Others who have benefitted from Colbert drives include Amnesty International, Autism Speaks, Feeding America, the Global Fund for Women, and Stand Up to Cancer. Finally, Colbert also donates all proceeds from his public appearances.

Why did he give so much? Christian charity? *Noblesse oblige*? "That we have the capacity to give so much of ourselves to others is, I think, what separates us humans from the animals," he said. "Sure, there are other things, like the fact that we don't shoot venom out of fangs."

"Colbert the Prankster" earned wild applause, and "Colbert the Philanthropist" won enduring gratitude. But "Colbert the Politician," despite his impishness and *joie de vivre*, drew venom from the powers that be. Beyond his roast of President Bush, Colbert rankled politicians of both parties. He was at his best, however, when taking on the universe of greed, ego, and cold cash that American politics now embodies.

In late 2007, responding to Internet petitions nominating Stewart and Colbert for president and vice president, Colbert threw his hat in the ring. He was not the first comedian to stage a mock run for the White House. In 1968, when Vietnam and race riots brought American politics to a boiling point, the deadpan comic Pat Paulsen ran a satiric campaign that included smoke-filled fund-raisers, whistle-stop tours, and speeches on *The Smothers Brothers Comedy Hour*. But Paulsen never filed papers to run for office, and he never appeared on any ballot. Even when he revived his campaign and received hundreds of write-in votes, Paulsen drew a line between satire and serious campaigning.

Colbert decided to erase that line. He announced his candidacy in a mid-October 2007 *Report*. Balloons fell from the ceiling, "I'M DOING IT!" flashed on the screen, and the audience all but wet themselves. Three days later, he appeared on *Meet the Press*. Host Tim Russert, unsure which Colbert was seated across from him, tried to be both straight man and comic. Challenging Colbert's last name, Russert asked if he should change his name to "Russ-air." But Colbert stayed in character, explaining why he was running.

"The junctures that we face are both critical and unforeseen, and the real challenge is how we will respond to these junctures, be they unprecedented or unforeseen, or, God help us, critical." Without his roaring studio audience, Colbert fell flat on *Meet the Press*. That Sunday afternoon, however, he flew to South Carolina's capital, Columbia, for his first rally. Before a cheering crowd, he announced, "I promise, if elected, I will crush the state of

Georgia." The Mayor of Columbia gave him a key to the city and proclaimed "Stephen Colbert Day." Polls soon showed Colbert backed by 2.3 percent of South Carolina voters, more than New Mexico's Governor Bill Richardson could muster.

Colbert continued milking the campaign on camera, but when he filed papers to be on the primary ballot in South Carolina, officials thought the joke had gone far enough. The executive council of the South Carolina Democratic Party convened to decide his fate. Before their meeting, Colbert lobbied the council with cocktails and snacks, shaking hands and "spoon feeding them Democratic talking points, most of which I lifted from Neil Young lyrics." The following day, the verdict was announced. "The council really agonized over this," said chairwoman Carol Fowler, "because they really like him, they love his show, and everyone thinks it's wonderful that he cares about us." But by a thirteen-to-three vote, Colbert's application was rejected. Claiming he was not a viable nationwide candidate, the council returned his $2,500 filing fee. Colbert broke down on camera. He would return.

In 2010, Colbert again crossed the line between comedy and politics. This time, his rejection was not so polite. That September, California Congresswoman Zoe Lofgren, whom Colbert had hosted on the *Report*, invited him to address a congressional committee debating an agricultural jobs bill. Colbert had already participated in a migrant workers' "Take Our Jobs Day," picking beans in upstate New York. He planned to tell Congress about the backbreaking labor, but would they take him seriously?

By then, the congressmen he once tricked into improv interviews knew him well. His show, books, and soaring celebrity had made him a household name, and he was just a month away from a rally with Jon Stewart on the Mall in Washington, D.C. Everyone, it seemed, loved Stephen Colbert, even Bill O'Reilly. "I think satire is very, very entertaining for any society to have," O'Reilly said of Colbert. "I have never had a problem with it as long as it's not mean-spirited, and I don't think he is." But if there is one entity whose members refuse to laugh, it is the United States Congress. So when Colbert sat down before the congressional subcommittee, he faced the toughest audience of his life.

On a sunny morning in late September in Washington, D.C., Room 2141 of the Rayburn House Office Building teemed with Colbert Nation citizens. Colbert entered with a police escort. One woman shouted, "Thank you for saving our corn, Stephen!" As cameramen snapped photos, the congressmen and women sat at their mikes bewildered or tight-lipped. Opening the hearing,

Rep. John Conyers of Michigan thanked Colbert for drawing so much attention and then asked Colbert to kindly excuse himself and let the committee get on with its business.

Colbert should have taken the advice. Instead, he deferred to the congresswoman who had invited him. Lofgren urged him to speak, and Colbert began by sharing "my vast experience spending one day as a migrant farm worker."

"Does one day in the field make you an expert witness?" a congressman asked.

"I believe that one day of me studying anything makes me an expert," Colbert replied.

He then gave a semi-serious, semi-satirical look at migrant work that drew few laughs and much scorn. Having picked beans for a day, he was shocked to discover that "most soil is at ground level." Joke after joke drew a chuckle or two from the gallery and glares from the congressmen.

"This is America," Colbert went on. "I don't want a tomato picked by a Mexican. I want it picked by an American, then sliced by a Guatemalan and served by a Venezuelan in a spa where a Chilean gives me a Brazilian." He received few laughs.

Colbert continued reading from a written statement: "Maybe the easier answer is to find fruits and vegetables that pick themselves. The scientists over at 'Fruit of the Loom' have made great strides in fruit-human hybrids." Silence merged with disgust.

Stepping out of character, Colbert said he had accepted Lofgren's invitation because "I like talking about people who don't have any power, and it seems like some of the least powerful people in the United States are migrant workers who come and do our work but don't have any rights themselves."

The congressmen remained resentful, and the press denounced Colbert's testimony as a "stunt" that was "emblematic of the dumbing-down of American political culture." *Colbert v. Congress* was not an Internet sensation. Even today, it's hard to watch.

Colbert's brief testimony had scarcely dumbed down American political culture, but by 2011, many wondered whether Colbert and Stewart were doing democracy any favors. Ever since "The Year of Jon Stewart" in 2004, media experts had worried that "fake news" might be harming young Americans who made up the bulk of *The Daily Show* audience.

Professors and pundits fretted. And in 2005, when *The Colbert Report* doubled the dosage, academic studies of Comedy Central's late-night duo proliferated. Were viewers learning anything from "soft news?" Did nightly viewing of Stewart and Colbert lead to negative perceptions of politicians? Were the two shows deepening the cynicism that many adults lamented as the default mode in today's youth? And in an age when John McCain appeared on *SNL*, side by side with Tina Fey as Sarah Palin, was there any such thing as fake news?

Initial studies warned that comedic news might alienate viewers from the political process. Gradually, however, a different consensus emerged. Rather than detaching their audiences, professors found that *The Daily Show* and *The Colbert Report* heightened political involvement. Regular viewers were better informed than viewers of other cable news and better able to discuss issues. More recently, media analysts have gone further, defining a "Stewart-Colbert Effect" that changed how news is perceived.

The distinction between "fake" and "real news" is meaningless, political scientists Mark K. McBeth and Randy S. Clemons argued. Both Stewart and Colbert interviewed real newsmakers. Both showed clips of real events. Both had been guests on serious political shows, and both were in the news themselves. So what was real and what was fake? Various studies showed that viewers could not laugh at a Stewart-Colbert fake story if they did not know the real story.

Some academics have compared Stewart and Colbert to "court jesters." Others saw them as savvy purveyors of that most cherished commodity, "cool." Being cynical and funny, they had become trustworthy, especially to the eighteen-to-forty-nine-year-old demographic whose loyalty they owned, according to late-night ratings. Yet Stewart and Colbert also offered a constructive alternative to a media that was increasingly polarized, polemical, and sometimes just inane.

Stewart and Colbert were not just ironic; they were intelligent and not just cool, but cerebral. No longer mere comics, Stewart and Colbert, one study said, were "*rhetorical critics . . .* who creatively guide audiences towards democratic possibilities." And their work, another professor claimed, could "arguably, be considered some of the most embracing and engaging commentary on the television landscape."

But one academic saw disturbing shifts in reality itself. The Stewart-Colbert effect, said Professor Robert J. Tally, Jr., was "hyper-reality." As defined by European theorists Jean Baudrillard and Umberto Eco, hyper-reality sets in when simulations are perceived to be no less real than the real thing. Disneyland, Las Vegas, wax museums, theme restaurants, faux castles, and fake dinosaurs – all are part of the American obsession with the "Absolute Fake." Stewart-Colbert and their "almost real" headlines were just another example of hyper-reality, Tally concluded. "Above all," he said, "these programs impress upon the viewers the profound sense that the mainstream media's real news is not much more real than its satirical or parodistic copies. Hence, the distinction between the real news and the fake news begins to recede."

Academics posit; professors profess. Colbert viewers had to decide for themselves whether they knew the difference between the fake and the real, and whether they cared. But the reality of *The Colbert Report* never got more hyper than during the 2012 presidential campaign. Expanding on his aborted 2008 run for the White House, Colbert obliterated the line between fake and real news. In the process, he bared the sheer hypocrisy of campaign finance, exposed the hype and greed, and won another Peabody.

It all started on Colbert's birthday, May 13, 2011, when he formed his own Super PAC, an independent political action committee. These committees had been popping up since the Supreme Court's *Citizens United* decision in 2010. What Citizen United did allowed unlimited corporate and union donations to the PACs, which could, in turn, funnel unlimited amounts of cash into any candidate's campaign so long as the PAC remained "independent" from candidates and their staffs. *Citizens United* was analyzed, protested, and embraced, but only Colbert took the hyper-real road of forming his own Super PAC.

As he had done in South Carolina, Colbert filed the necessary papers to participate in the process. Inside the Washington, D.C., office of the Federal Election

Commission, Colbert faced down an official who thought he was joking. "Hadn't he been kidding when he appeared before Congress?" Colbert stood his ground. His congressional testimony was "a completely different issue," he said. "This is something I'm asking for. It's a right as described by the *Citizens United* case. And I believe that the *Citizens United* decision was the right one. There should be unlimited corporate money, and I want some of it. I don't want to be the one chump who doesn't have it."

After deliberating, the FEC ruled, by a five-to-one vote, in favor of Colbert. Colbert Super PAC, later renamed Americans for a Better Tomorrow, Tomorrow, began soliciting funds. The solicitation began on the sidewalk outside the FEC's office. Standing on a platform, Colbert told a few hundred fans that he was not joking. Participating in democracy was not funny. But he did have one Super PAC joke.

"Knock knock!"

"Who's there?" the crowd responded.

"Unlimited union and corporate campaign contributions."

"Unlimited union and corporate campaign contributions who?"

"That's the thing," Colbert said. "I don't think I should have to tell you."

Why form a Super PAC? Colbert was asked. His answer: the American Dream. "And that dream is simple. That anyone, no matter who they are, if they are determined, if they are willing to work hard enough, someday they could grow up to create a legal entity which could then receive unlimited corporate funds, which could be used to influence our elections."

Wrapping up his talk, Colbert said, "I don't accept the status quo, but I do accept Visa, MasterCard, or American Express." He then circulated through the crowd gathering credit cards that he swiped into an iPad. "Anybody else got a credit card?" he asked. "Is there any more cash? Just ball it up and throw it at me!"

Come August, when GOP candidates began stumping in Iowa for its upcoming straw poll, Colbert was toying with reality as no comedian ever had. First, Americans for a Better Tomorrow, Tomorrow funded a TV ad urging Iowans to write in "Rick Parry, Parry with an 'A,' not Rick Perry, the Texas governor that other PACs were supporting. The 'A' stands for America and for IowA," the ad said. Replete with images of dollar bills raining down on cornfields, Colbert's faux ad ran on two TV stations in Des Moines.

No one knows how many write-in votes Rick Parry got, but Colbert's Super PAC rolled on into the fall with 165,000 members. "I know of some of my peers whose first political contribution (and probably last) was to Colbert's Super PAC," a student in Florida said.

Taking the absurdity up a notch, Colbert formed a Citizens United hybrid that allowed him to accept anonymous donations. According to the latest campaign laws, "Colbert Super PAC SHH" could even divert anonymous donations into his regular PAC. Colbert insisted that his super mockery was "100 percent legal and at least 10 percent ethical," but to make sure, he hired an actual campaign finance lawyer. Trevor Potter, former FEC chairman, began consulting Colbert on and off camera.

The press, as disgusted as Colbert by the billions flowing through campaign coffers, lapped up his every move. "It's as though Jonathan Swift took his satirical suggestion about Irish babies one step further and actually cooked one," *The New York Times* wrote. Media analysts were amazed that anyone could make politics seem more transparently absurd than it had become. "I am much taken by this and can't think of any real parallel in history," said Stephen Hess of the Brookings Institution. "Yes, comedians have always told jokes about elections, but this is quite different. This is a funny person being very serious, actually talking about process. What comedian talks about process?"

In January 2012, as the primary campaign loomed, Colbert again targeted South Carolina. First, he offered $500,000 to the GOP if it would rename the primary, "The Colbert Super PAC South Carolina Republican Party." No one took him seriously, so he upped the ante. He entered the primary. This time he was allowed into the game, but with a catch. "You cannot be a candidate and run a Super PAC," his lawyer told him on the show. "That would be coordinating with yourself." "Right," Colbert responded, "and I'd go blind."

Needing a new Super PAC coordinator, Colbert turned to Jon Stewart. Early in January, Colbert traveled the few blocks from his studio to Stewart's to make the move. Seated across a desk, the two men bumped fists, then pressed them together. Both shuddered as glowing, green dollar signs passed from Colbert's body into Stewart's. An announcer boomed, "Colbert Super PAC Transfer–*ACTIVATE!*" The "Definitely-Not-Coordinated-with-Stephen Colbert Super PAC" was open for donations.

For the next two months, Stewart and Colbert shredded Super PACs and their supposed independence. Appearing again on *The Daily Show*, Colbert called his lawyer. "Hello, Trevor," Colbert said. "I'm sitting here with Jon Stewart."

"Oh, but don't worry," Stewart chimed in. "We're not . . ." and both men chorused, "coordinating!" Stewart began suggesting campaign strategies. To each, Colbert, grinning or frowning, repeated, "I cannot coordinate with you in any way."

The spoof concluded with the men agreeing it had been great "NOT coordinating with you." The ongoing joke even charmed candidates – one, at least. Herman Cain did not mind when Colbert joined the Republican's bus tour of South Carolina. "Anyone who finds what Mr. Colbert is doing offensive should simply lighten up," Cain said.

When Cain later withdrew his candidacy after charges that he had had an affair, Colbert became Cain. Americans for a Better Tomorrow, Tomorrow ran ads in South Carolina, featuring Colbert campaigning as its voice-over and urging viewers to vote for Herman Cain.

By the end of January, Colbert's Super PAC had raked in a million dollars in contributions. "To all the worrywarts out there who said Super PACs were going to lead to a cabal of billionaires secretly buying democracy," Colbert said, "Wrong! They are *publicly* buying democracy."

Evolving daily, Colbert's Super PAC took political satire to new heights. Colbert, wrote *Ad Age*, had become the "greatest living cultural/media critic. . . . There is no funnier or smarter (or more heartbreaking or depressing) deconstruction of the American scene - particularly our fatally-flawed political process, as signified by Colbert's Super PAC - to be found anywhere else in the culture right now."

When it was all over, Colbert got serious. Even after buying ads for Herman Cain, Americans for a Better Tomorrow, Tomorrow was left with more than $700,000. Colbert did what he always does with excess money: He gave it away, dividing the fund equally among Hurricane Sandy relief, Habitat for Humanity, Donors Choose, and two other charities. And in April 2012, Colbert's spoof won the Peabody Award.

In 2012, Colbert contracted to continue his show through the end of 2014. Entering that year, with ratings steady and his Nation as loyal as ever, he looked likely to commit to the show for the long term. Then on April 10, 2014, CBS executives announced that their replacement for the departing David Letterman would be Stephen Colbert. The news made headlines in every entertainment section of every newspaper and magazine. Colbert's future rivals in late-night television, comedians Jimmy Kimmel and Jimmy Fallon, heaped praise on Colbert. "A finer or funnier man I do not know," Kimmel tweeted while Fallon chimed in, calling Colbert "a genius, the funniest man alive." Others were less enthusiastic. Noting Colbert's mockery of conservatives, radio host Rush Limbaugh said CBS had "declared war on the heartland of America." Colbert, however, quickly announced that his blowhard persona would not host *CBS Late Night with Stephen Colbert*.

Within a few hours of CBS' announcement, Colbert went on the air to tell his Nation the news. He began with effusive praise for Letterman, then said, "I gotta tell ya, I do *not* envy whoever they try to put in that chair." The audience burst into applause, chanting "Ste-phen, Ste-phen, Ste-phen!" When the tumult faded, Colbert continued. "Those are some huge shoes to fill," he said, "and some really big pants."

In the week following the announcement, Colbert seemed happier than anyone. He appeared on *The Daily Show*, telling a mock-shocked Jon Stewart that he was leaving because "there's no mountain left for me to climb – it's become clear to me that I have won television." Again dodging direct mention of the move, he suggested he would "go wherever the wind takes me, Jon, maybe ride the rails, live boxcar to boxcar, learn how to whip up a hearty stew from peanut shells and a stolen chicken." When Stewart suggested he stay in television, noting that Letterman was retiring, Colbert replied, "Yes, I heard that too, Jon, but they already gave the part to some fat guy." Then he showed a clip of his early years on the *Daily Show* and said, "I'm really going to miss me."

The following night, Colbert appeared on Letterman's show. Looking professorial in a black suit and horn-rimmed glasses, Colbert played it straight. He assured Letterman that he was "thrilled" by the move, then Colbert told a little-known story about having been hired over his girlfriend as a *Late Night* intern in 1986. He turned the internship down because it did not pay. "This next job I'm taking here," he asked Letterman. "It pays, right? Because I already signed." Later he revealed that in 1997, when his career was floundering, he and Paul Dinello had applied to be *Late Night* writers. By the time Letterman's staff arranged an interview, however, *Strangers with Candy* had begun filming, and Colbert didn't need a job.

Having made the news official, Colbert spent the summer as if there were no end to his split personality. Only in late October did he finalize the move, using a *Colbert Report* opening to announce the date of his last show. This time he did not soften the blow. After pitching the paperback version of his book *America Again*, Colbert urged viewers to buy it because "on December 18, my show is ending." Groans filled the audience who knew that, finally, this was no joke. "The point is, Stephen Colbert, the guy you've seen here every night for nine years, will be gone. And all you'll have left of me is this book . . ."

The Colbert Report ended. But the real Stephen Colbert, the fifty-year-old father of three, patron of the arts, philanthropist, and New Jersey commuter is still with us. The master improv artist from Second City, the sketch comedian from the 90s returned to television. In making his bold move, Colbert deftly fended off the fate of too many comedians. Class clowns turned professional comics have a disturbing tendency to burn out or rust, to become happy-faced "humorists" or bitter curmudgeons. Stephen Colbert chose a different route, one worthy of his persona: character suicide.

He killed the bloviating, self-promoting egomaniac once known as the president of Colbert Nation. Looking back at the show's nine years, it's clear that Stephen Colbert did more than make us laugh. He changed the way Americans perceive the truth. And truth, once its definition is changed, is never quite the same.

What, then, is truthiness? Is it just, as Colbert once said, "a word I pulled right out of my keister?" Is it the human weakness of believing whatever half-truths one finds convenient? Is truthiness personal reality? Hyper-reality? Whatever becomes "real" because enough people say it's real? Or are all attempts to pin down truthiness rendered futile by its nature?

Truthiness, it turns out, came from Colbert's keister because it describes his life. No ordinary word could sum up a life that turned tragedy into fantasy, fantasy into improv, improv into parody, parody into satire, and finally satire into comedic superstardom. Likewise, no reality-based lexicon could explain how a kid from South Carolina could go from brooding nerd to comic foil and from "high status idiot" to "greatest living cultural/media critic." Nothing but truthiness could do justice to the contradictions within Stephen Colbert. Nothing else could span the gap between his egomania on camera and his gentleness off camera, nor highlight the contrast between the tight-fisted politics he pretends to embrace and the generous principles he lives by. Truthiness? It's not just the Word of the Day. It is the word of Stephen Colbert's life. But he deserves the last word.

"Knock knock. Who's there? The Truth. No joke."

SOURCES

about.com, http://politicalhumor.about.com/cs/ quotethis/a/reagan quotes.htm

AdAge, Jan. 30, 2012.

Amarasingam, Arnarnat, *The Stewart-Colbert Effect: Essays on the Real Impacts of Fake News,* McFarland, New York 2011, p. 128.

American Dialect Society, "Truthiness Voted Word of the Year," http//www.americandialect.org/ Words_of_the_Year_2005.pdf

Atlanta Journal-Constitution, May 8, 2006.

Atlantic Monthly, http://www.theatlanticwire.com/ entertainment/2011/05/ stephen-colbert-federal-election-commission/37731/

Brainyquote.com

Buffalo News, March 30, 2008

Chicago Daily Herald, Jan. 20, 2012.

Chicago Reader, July 9, 1992; April 14, 1994.

Chicago Sun-Times, Sept. 21, 1995.

Chicago Tribune, Jan. 18, 2006.

CNN.com, May 6, 2004.

Colbertnation.com

Daily Mail.co.UK

thedailyshow.cc.com

Eco, Umberto, *Travels in Hyper-reality: Essays*, Harcourt, San Diego, New York, London, 1986, pp. 20-21.

Hollywood Reporter, Oct. 31, 2005.

Houston Chronicle, Nov. 7, 2005.

Ign.com, "Interview with Stephen Colbert."

Jezebel.com

Los Angeles Daily News, July 28, 2003; Oct. 31, 2005.

Montgomery County (CA) Herald, Oct. 30, 2007.

National Traffic Safety Board, "Air Accident Report 75-9," May 23, 1975. http://www.airdisaster.com/

reports/ntsb/AAR75-09.pdf

New York Daily News, Jan. 18, 2007; Sept. 25, 2010.

New York Times, Feb. 8, 1995; Oct. 25, 1997; Aug. 12, 1998; April 30, 1999; Aug. 27, 2004; Oct. 27, 2004; Oct. 12, 2005; Jan. 22, 2006; Nov. 5, 2006; May 8, 2006; Nov. 2, 2007; May 7, 2009; Sept. 25, 2010; Oct. 13, 2010; Aug. 22, 2011.

New York Times Magazine: Jan. 4, 2012.

notablebiographies.com   http://www.notablebiographies.com/newsmakers2/2007-A-Co/Colbert-Stephen.html

Oed.com

Onion AV Club, Jan. 22, 2003.

oprah.com

http://www.oprah.com/own-oprahs-next-chapter/The-Love-of-Stephen-Colberts-Life-Video.

Philadelphia Daily News, Oct. 18, 2005; July 1, 2011.

Philadelphia Inquirer, May 7, 2006.

Pittsburgh Post-Gazette, Aug. 9, 2006.

Playboy, November 12. [COMPLETE DATE AND PAGE?]

Rogak, Lisa, *And Nothing But the Truthiness: The Rise (and Further Rise) of Stephen Colbert,* St. Martin's

Press, New York, NY 2011, pp. 32-33, 36, 41, 58, 64, 77, 80, 86, 94, 100, 107, 116, 119, 124, 145, 153, 156, 160, 163, 182, 187, 189, 200.

Rolling Stone, March 23, 1995; Nov. 16, 2006.

San Antonio Express-News, May 29, 2006.

San Francisco Chronicle, May 1, 2006.

San Francisco Chronicle podcast, Jan. 16, 2006.

Seattle Post-Intelligencer, Oct. 27, 2005; May 6, 2006.

60 Minutes, YouTube.com

splitsider.com

http://splitsider.com/2011/06/stephen-colbert-on-his-relationship-with-jon-stewart/

Spolin, Viola, *Improvisation for the Theatre: 3E,* Northwestern University Press, Evanston, IL, 1999, pp. xiii, xiv.

squidoo.com

http://www.squidoo.com/stephen-colbert-charity

Tampa Bay Times, May 16, 2012.

Thomas, Mike, *The Second City Unscripted: Revolution and Revelation at the World-Famous Comedy Theater,* Villard, New York, 2009, p. xi, 200, 201, 208, 209, 210.

USA Today, April 7, 1999; May 4, 2005; Oct. 14, 2005;

Oct. 31, 2005; Nov. 21, 2008.

Vanity Fair, October 2007.

Variety, Jan. 20, 2009.

Washington Post, May 4, 2006; Aug. 6, 2006; Sept. 29, 2010.

YouTube.com

Made in the USA
Columbia, SC
11 December 2019

84683881R00078